Desktop Follies

Abandon hype all ye who enter here.

For Neil
who taught me
all I know—
except how to
proofread
Fran

Desktop Follies

Frank J. Romano

GAMA

Why you would want to reproduce this stuff is beyond me.

GAMA
PO Box 170
Salem, NH 03079
603-898-2822
fxrppr@rit.edu

First Edition: October 1999
Printed in the United States of America
by Malloy Lithographing

ISBN: 0-93853-01-5

Introduction

I attend more meetings, conferences, seminars, symposia, colloquia, briefings, presentations, and sessions than anyone else I know, other than Larry Warter of Fuji. I speak at many of them and sit in the audience and listen to the pundits at the podium. As a result, I have time—perhaps too much time—to reflect on their words and ideas and just stuff in general.

So for many years I printed the little jottings that I made during these periods in a column in *TypeWorld* and later *Electronic Publishing* magazine called *Frank Talk*. After a while, this became an outlet for all manner of one-liners, tidbits, comments, reflections, musings, and bad poetry.

Some of the material is original and some is borrowed and adapted. You will note that certain subjects come up constantly. For a while the hype about desktop-this and desktop-that was a little overwhelming. My eternal vendetta with the typeface Souvenir continues.

The illustrations are all by Bob Glueckstein, a retired cartoonist from Menonomee Falls, Wisconsin, who contributed these little gems for many years to the publication. Many were done in the early Eighties, so Bob was truly ahead of his time.

Frank Romano
October, 1999

About the author

Frank Romano's career has spanned over 33 years in the printing and publishing industries. He is the author of over thirty books, co-author of the International Paper *Pocket Pal,* contributor to major encyclopedias and dictionaries, and the author of numerous articles.

His most recent books are "Pocket Guide to Digital Prepress," "PDF Printing & Publishing" (with four RIT students), and the 10,000-term "Encyclopedia of Graphic Communications" (with Richard Romano).

He has founded eight publications, serving as publisher or editor or both for *TypeWorld* now *Electronic Publishing* which is in its 22nd year of publication, *Computer Artist, Color Publishing, The Typographer, EP&P,* and both the *NCPA* and *PrintRIT Journals.*

He lectures extensively throughout the United States and Canada, having addressed virtually every club, association, group and professional organization at one time or another.

He has consulted for major corporations, publishers, government and other users of digital publishing technology.

He has been quoted in the *New York Times, Wall Street Journal, Times* of London, *USA Today, Business Week,* and many other newspapers and publications, as well as on TV and radio.

Professor Romano now teaches digital publishing, and digital printing at the Rochester Institute of Technology, College of Imaging Arts and Sciences.

Table of Contents

Requiem for the Typewriter

Smith Corona Corp. filed bankruptcy. It was the last maker of typewriters in the United States.

Other kids usually want dolls, model trains, or bikes as gifts. As a kid, I wanted a typewriter. In 1957 my parents gave me a Royal portable typewriter. It was white and had a smell of ink from the ribbon and lubricating oil from the key bars that stayed with it for years. It was the greatest gift I ever received (other than my two sons).

The deal was made that I had to improve my handwriting in the year before. My parents feared that I would somehow forget how to write once I started typing.

As a self-taught typist I still type with two fingers—actually one and a half fingers. I still have to look at the both the keys and the computer screen and this is getting harder with bifocals.

There was no correcting system in 1957. You erased an error with one of those round red erasers with a little brush on the end. Every few years you cleaned the eraser droppings out from between the type bars. Later they had long thin gray erasers but the round red ones were a required peripheral...and you could write your name around it.

If you wanted a copy there was a miracle product called carbon paper. If you used it and made a mistake, you had twice the erasing to do. I once had a job that required 10 copies and you better believe that I was a careful typist. The last carbon copy was a pale ghost of gray.

You tried not to make too many mistakes. Fortunately, the mechanical nature of the system required some effort to depress the key. This was a de facto method for slowing you down. For important correspondence, typists did encounter what was called "end of page pressure"—the stress of realizing that an error at the beginning could be fixed by starting over again without much investment in the document, but an error near the end required starting over and redoing a lot more.

Of course, after fifty lines at double spacing the last word would be going downhill as the paper shifted in the platen.

That wonderful old Royal got me through six plus

years of college at night. When I got a job I was given a "new" Royal typewriter, circa 1940. It was black and majestic and all mine. I worked with it for seven years and when I visited the company 15 years later, it was still there . . . with the same ribbon, I think.

I do not recall anyone ever complaining about repetitive stress injury even though operating a mechanical typewriter gave you the biceps of Hulk Hogan. There was that joyful sense of accomplishment as you completed a line and sent the carriage back to the beginning of the left margin.

There was no bold or italic, so you underlined, or typed all caps or typed a character and then backspaced and typed it again to give the illusion of boldface. Centering required mental calculation to add the characters and deduct them from the total line and then space over to start. Miss a space and you were in trouble.

The spacebar was your cursor and more. It controlled all indents and spacing. This was possible, of course, because of the mono spaced character set. Every character was the same width.

In 1980 I wrote a book called "Machine Writing and Typesetting" and it traced the early history of the typewriter and the Linotype. Let me reminisce with you about those halcyon days before word processing.

Enter Sholes

Christopher Latham Sholes was the 52nd person to invent the typewriter, but the only one to call it that. He was a newspaper publisher in Wisconsin and an amateur inventor. He had read about a mechanical writing device in an issue of the "Scientific American" and decided to invent such a device as a means of setting type.

He was fortunate that a new material, called carbon paper, had just come into use in telegraph offices. He used some printer's type, put it on a crude key mechanism and typed a row of W's. He realized that he needed a few more keys to make it a success.

Sholes finally developed a crude machine and then started looking for investors. Without getting into detail, he found one who turned out to be a charlatan, but who did accomplish the deal with the Remington Arms Company to manufacture the device. By then Sholes had sold all his rights to the typewriter. No one really remembers him. The city of Milwaukee once named a park after him, but years later no one remembered why and the name of the park was changed.

His daughter was the first operator as such and paved the way for women to enter the business world. Before the typewriter most secretaries were male. The keyboard was hard to learn but it has endured to this day as the standard, even though it is illogical. Supposedly Sholes laid the keyboard out to avoid the keys hitting each other at moderate typing speeds. I still believe that he was left handed and positioned the keys for his own comfort, thus getting even for all southpaws that will ever live.

Interestingly, the top line of characters spells out "typewriter." Well, plus a few other letters.

The first author ever to use a typewriter was Mark Twain. He and his friend, columnist Petroleum Nasby, were walking along a street in Boston and saw the typewriter in a store window. Twain describes the episode in his "Autobiography." The demonstrator typed "The boy stood on the burning deck…" at high speed and Twain bought it on the spot to convert from writing long hand to typing.

But he could never get the speed and believed that there was only one line the demonstrator knew by heart in order to fake the speedy demo. It is said that he sent the first typed manuscript to a publisher who wrote back that he left out the punctuation. Twain is said to have sent a sheet with periods, commas, etc with a note to insert them wherever necessary.

Enter Clephane

Now the story gets interesting. A guy named Clephane made the statement "I want to bridge the gap between the typewriter and the printed page." He made it in 1876. He thought that he could put lithographic ink on the typewriter ribbon and type a sheet and then transfer the image to a litho stone. He met a man named Ottmar Mergenthaler who convinced hin that relief metal was the only way to mechanize typesetting and the typewriter was abandoned as a typesetting device and the linotype was born in 1886 to revolutionize the printing industry.

There were many attempts to bring the typewriter and

the typesetter together. The Hammond typewriter became the Varityper with proportional type, as did the Friden Justowriter and the IBM Composer. These machines created the "cold type" revolution of the 1960's before phototypesetting really succeeded.

Enter IBM

In the 1930's IBM bought the Electrographic Typewriter Company and sold the first electric device. While mechanical typewriter makers had to convert their plants for war manufacturing, IBM's electric devices were deemed more productive for all those clerks doing the paperwork for military men and women.

In 1961 the Selectric typewriter gave us the "golf ball" mechanism which was unique in that the key did not actuate a mechanical action but rather generated a code which selected the character and then activated impression. That made it easy for IBM to send that code to a magnetic tape and then back to the print head. Word processing was born. And for many years, even their word processing competitors used the Selectric typewriter mechanism for their keyboard and printer.

In 1972 I was among the first to use a Redactron word processor. Later on I sent a magnetic tape cassette of an article to *Folio* magazine as the first magazine to receive and input an article without re-keying it from the typewritten manuscript. In the late 70's daisy wheels and other mechanisms competed with the ever popular golf ball typewriter.

By then I had an IBM Selectric and still do. My wife still uses it to type envelopes and labels. The repair person died last year, so when it breaks that will be it for this trusty machine. I will probably put it in the garage and it will stay there until my estate is probated and someone will finally bring it to the landfill. I won't.

In 1956, Texas secretary Bette Nesmith Graham invented Liquid Paper and made a fortune, which she left to her son Michael Nesmith, of the rock group *The Monkees*. White-Out will go down in history as the single most important advance in civilization. As laser and ink jet printers enter the market it will also be a tool of the past and Mike will have to go back to singing.

To this day I think my best work came from that Selectric. Like others, I would plan an article in my mind or even outline it on paper. Then I would type it in one fell swoop with almost no changes. Today I stare at a screen and then start typing, go back and edit and edit. I am more apt to try to proofread on the screen rather than the printed page as I used to. I know I caught more problems that way. The new way may be flashy and modern, but the old way was better.

Spell checking? It was proofreading and a dictionary. I and many others always had one handy. I often found a better word while checking a word and probably expanded my vocabulary. Electronic spell checkers are more of a nuisance than anything else.

Enter the PC

In 1981 I made the leap into desktop computing with an IBM PC-XT and a NEC daisywheel printer. I kept my Selectric nearby for moral support. We all started with Wordstar in those days and then switched to Multimate. Later on it was Xywrite, the best editorial tool ever.

In 1984 it became the Macintosh and I felt comfortable with typographic formats. I lived through the Imagewriter and jumped at the Laserwriter. I still use QuarkXPress as a word processor so I don't have to learn another program like Word or Word Perfect. I know I often spend more time on the look of the document rather than the content.

The typewriter had almost no format capability so you had to concentrate on the content.

Exit Smith Corona

The relentless march of progress touches everything in its path. I hope it's progress. And maybe sentiment is supposed to yield to progress.

I do not believe that today's computers will have the life span of the typewriter or the ease of use, or the nostalgia. I do not feel nostalgic for my old Kaypro. Computers are changed every few years, but typewriters were kept for a lifetime.

Royal, Remington, IBM, and Smith Corona don't make typewriters any more. They said that computers did them in because computers had memories and typewriters did not. Fortunately, typewriter *users* have memories.

Random Bits

What if you could print the CD-ROM? Instead of stamping them out, we could print the recorded data on new kinds of stock.

Intel has a chip that issues a billion instructions a second. I know a Marine Drill Instructor like that.

A new inkjet printer has permanent ink but the machine fades away.

There was a guy sitting on the sidewalk with an old laptop computer and a sign "Will set type for RAM." I gave him two bits.

The sign said "hands on" demos. Demos should be "hands off."

After plastic surgery comes Photoshop surgery. Enhance your edges. Remove any under color. Replace your gray component. Change your image by changing your image.

There was actually a printing press at a recent publishing event, considering that many exhibits were for products that would eliminate printing. Of course, they all had printed literature.

I put a flea and tick collar on my wrist and now my watch only goes tock tock.

Life was simpler once, like when America belonged to the Indians and there was only one Zip code: 1.

Sub-atomic delusion
And fusion confusion
Caused a negative reaction
By the fission faction
With continuing conviction
Of friction fiction

My reality check bounced.

Deep Thoughts on Einstein

Einstein first supported and then rejected the Atomic Bomb. He thought it would destroy humanity. But he did not know much about television.

Saw a recent PBS special on Albert Einstein. The show was not as good as the subject, relatively speaking.

Einstein said that if you go fast enough in one direction you will go backward in time. Sort of like mankind.

No wonder Amtrak is always late.

This means that if fast food is fast enough you can burp before you bite.

The speed of light is one area the Postal Service will never have to worry about. The speed of dark?

When Einstein came to America
He crossed a cruel dark sea
He found a universe of time and space
And called it relativity

Until the day he died, Einstein was at work on a unified field theory for the inter-relationship of all the forces of the universe—light, gravity, magnetism, peer pressure, distress of the lower tract, and static cling.

The Galactic Paradoxes

1. Taking a picture of a scanner with a digital camera.
2. Scanning a photo of a scanner.
3. Photographing a digital image on a screen.
4. Trying to figure what it all means.

A complex system that does not work, invariably evolved from a simple system that did work.

If you take the low res
And I take the high res
I'll get to print it before you.

Under precisely controlled experimental conditions, a laboratory animal will do what it darn well wants to do.

System delusion: the misguided assumption that systems actually perform as advertised.

What has a gigabyte of on-line information, text and graphic, a friendly and universal user interface, immediate and random access, high levels of portability and full annotation capability? A newspaper. A magazine. A book.

Print—what a concept.

Wang once said there would be paperless offices. Now there are Wangless offices.

DNA is just protoplasmic pixels.

DNA: Style sheets for organisms.

A digital ice cream bar is a popsixel.

An up-and-coming pixel is a pixelette.

Full grown, they're pixelves.

Concept—what a concept.

They're know miss steaks in this copy cause we used special soft wear witch checks yore spelling. It is mower or lass a weigh too verify. How ever is can knot correct arrows inn punctuation ore usage: an it will not fined words witch are miss used butt spelled rite. Four example; a paragraph could have mini flaws but wood bee past by the spell checker. And it wont catch the sentence fragment which you. Their fore, the massage is that proofreading is knot eliminated, it is still berry much reek wired.

The History of the Typo

The history of the lowly typographical error is inexorably linked to the history of humankind. No other species is known to make typos. (Although hippopotami are known to make hippos.) A typo must involve type. Without type, there cannot be a typo. Pictures with errors are pictos. Thus the typo was born with the invention of typographic communication.

The ancient Koreans—not the Chinese—developed the process of block printing. It is said that a queen was near death and the high priests ordered the writing of a prayer in great number on small sheets of rice paper, probably printed with soy ink—the first edible printing. Technology came to the rescue and reproduced thousands of them—the first printed correspondence with a deity other than the 10 Commandments. The queen died anyway.

The Koreans were renowned for the quality of their work. There were even manuals for novices and journeymen. For instance, if a novice made one typo they lost a finger. The second typo caused the loss of a hand. This explains their reputation for quality...and the difficulty in recruiting new printers.

Centuries later, monks who spent their lives in scriptoria scribbling their way to Heaven also made mistakes. One wonders what profanity they uttered as they lost control of their quill pen. Was the name of the Saviour invoked for other reasons? To correct the error they could scrape away the ink from the vellum, which was the hide of a calf. Another method was to cover the error with a white paste and then write over it—the invention of White-Out, or in this case, Vellum-Out. In some cases, given the value of vellum, entire sheets were covered with medieval White-Out and used again. These are called palimpscests and archeologists often find that what was covered was more historically significant. I wonder if that will be true for modern memos. Or publications with articles like this.

Charlemagne standardized all writing throughout the Holy Roman Empire with an uncial writing style that would eventually be known as lowercase, designed by Alcuin of York, a British consultant. They could not standardize typographical errors, however, and individuality still prevailed, accounting for the breakup of the Empire into nationalistic state, each with its own handwriting style.

Gutenberg's secrecy was a marketing strategy. He wanted to sell mass-produced books at custom-produced prices. The Gutenbergian system of printing divided language into its basic building blocks—letters. Yet, the first work to be printed by moveable type was not a Bible, but rather an Indulgence, a sort of passport to Heaven, or more accurately, a form. Technologies may change, but bureaucracy endures.

After production of the first batch of Bibles, Gutenberg's erstwhile partner Johann Fust took several to Paris to sell. Since Bibles did not come on the market very often, their purchasers compared them. They found the same errors on the same pages. This had to be the work of the devil. Johann Fust died in Paris during that trip.

Now the opportunity for error was fully formed. Since copy had to be converted into type, the printer could easily select the wrong piece of metal. A new profession was born—the corrector of the press, today known as the proofreader. Their sole duty was to find mistakes before they got into print. Finding them afterward, did not count. Aldus Manutius, who almost single-handed created the Renaissance, used the philosopher Erasmus as a proofreader, as the great Greek and Latin texts were put into print for the first time, and thus were available to a wider audience.

The Gutenbergian font of 292 letters and letter combinations was reduced over the centuries. But humankind had no problem adapting—they just increased the number of errors per character.

The handset type methodology did not change for a few hundred years. A print shop after the Civil War used the same techniques that Gutenberg used.

It was an act of graphic vandalism that almost destroyed Mark Twain. The first edition of "Huck Finn" had been printed and the handset type re-distributed. On one of the engravings (illustrations) someone had scratched an image that made it obscene. The pages had not only been printed, they were partially bound. The entire run had to be discarded and production re-started. Combined with his investment in the failed Paige "typesetting machine" he was virtually wiped out financially.

Handset type yielded to linecasting. And a new error crept in—the wrong font. We could now mechanize our errors. Linecaster operators could not abort a line of type once started in the assembling elevator. Sensing an error, they would run their fingers down the first two rows of keys to produce ETAOIN SHRDLU which would be identified as a line to be discarded. However, the history of the newspaper industry reports that these lines often made their way into print and a generation of readers often asked "Who" or "What" was ETAOIN SHRDLU?

Linecasting was responsible for more errors than any other technology. In addition to keying errors there was also the mix up of lines during the page assembly process. Very often linecaster operators would communicate with their buddies at the "stone"—the assembly area—by sending notes on slugs. Too often, these found their way into print.

Paper tape and the TeleTypeSetter system allowed us to telecommunicate our typos to multiple sites at the same time. You no longer had to be present to see your errors in print.

Photographic typesetting came after 1960 and was combined with computer automation. Ah, the computer. Now we could automate our typos. However, phototype had its own unique aspects. Early keyboards required that the inputter type blind with no visual feedback. Later, one-line character and line displays were provided and then full video screens.

This gave rise to the electronic editorial system which eliminated all the people between the editor and the typesetting machine. Copy was no longer re-keyboarded, but editors found a way to maintain the same volume of typographical errors. In some cases, because of the lack of checks and balances provided by the division of labor skills, typos increased.

Computer hyphenation and justification was, and may still be, imperfect. It generated new and unique types of typos as words were broken with the worst possible resulting effect. Text processing entered the business office and changed forever the traditional typing process. A typist would begin typing on their Royal, Remington or IBM Selectric. An error in the first few lines would necessitate retyping from the beginning, but as they made their way down the page, their deodorant was tested by what IBM called "end of page pressure." The typewriter eraser—remember those round red erasers with little brushes on the end?—left droppings in the typewriter that resembled rubberized bat guano.

Then came White-Out and nirvana was achieved. Some typists used a 2-inch paint brush; some used a roller; some had it on tap.

But video-based word processing provided a degree of visual error correction—with the backspace, the delete and the change/find functions—and thus the typewriter, the White-Out and the eraser faded from the scene. Soon the PC became the de fact word processor that gave us memos faster, if not better.

Enter the most insidious technology ever created, capable of destroying the mental and moral fiber of our nation—the spelling checker. It can only find words that are absolutely wrong, but if the error creates an acceptable word—albeit an incorrect word—the checker does not know. Thus, more errors are creeping—no, galloping—into print.

One day I activated my spelling and grammar checkers, synonym finder (it still has not found a synonym for thesaurus), pomposity evaluator (why is abbreviate such a long word?), and sexist changer (it changes *mail man* to *person person*)—the machine hummed for a while and then flashed back the message "I think, therefore I am." With all that, at least it could have been more memorable.

Today artificial intelligence and fuzzy logic are being used to electronically generate typographical errors without human involvement. Mega-mip speeds and gigabyte storage combined with computers will supposedly find errors before they occur. Some computers are so fast, they can send typos back in time.

Imagine if you will a day when computers check your grammar, spelling and even the validity of your thoughts. They may have to generate artificial errors through a misspelling checker to appear more human.

But no matter what the computer does, typos are still the last vestige of human kind, for "To err is human" as each mistake validates our humanity.

Thus, we celebrate the typo.

Paper

Paper pushers cause paper addiction. It all starts innocently enough as you begin you decline into addiction with any old 20 pound xerographic bond. Pretty soon you're into 24 pound laser paper and then ...gasp...tinted stocks, especially goldenrod.

In no time you sink deeper into the depravity of woves and linen weaves and you start looking for watermarks. You're hooked. You have a ream on you back. Your brain is turning to pulp. You are a paper junkie.

What should you call recycled paper that's been recycled? Bi-cycled paper?

The Paperwork Reduction Act has helped to reduce bureaucratic document storage. Offices may now destroy old files so long as they copy them first.

Now that they have non-copyable paper, how about non-recordable disks or non-visible screens...or better yet, non-audible politicians?

Can you picture a world where workers have no paper on their desks. Scary. Instead of paper pushers, they would be byte jugglers.

One government agency is so secret, it makes artificial copies with white carbon paper.

Hammermill should produce a paper that already has type on it. You just white out the letters you don't want.

Printing papers are rising in price so quickly that forgers are bleaching the green from our currency because the paper is worth more.

I am still working on edible printing using rice paper and soy ink. Using various mixtures of ink and nutrients we can actually print the picture of the food and its taste. Watermelon is a problem because of pits on the plates.

Paper: something very complex for something very simple.

The conference we attended was in praise of paper, the real multimedium. You can file it, fold it, stick it in your pocket, carry it, annotate it, circulate it, mail it for only 33 cents, and a few hundred years from now someone will actually be able to read it.

Do you realize that there has never been paper on Star Trek's Enterprise? Of course, Captain Picard has the computer produce a very old book every now and then.

Can we dream of a time when there will be no paper? Sure. We could have very low cost, lightweight, portable display screens. But then there would be a time capsule with printed products from a bygone age.

What paper does the secret service use? Bond. James Bond.

In The Beginning, There Was TypeWorld

It was never expected that the publication we started in 1977 would survive to a 20th anniversary. The fact that it ever made it to a 10th was amazing. For a long time it was not pretty or well edited. It saw formidable competitors come and go, and like the homily says, the meek prevailed. It was never in the league of *Forbes* magazine but it put five kids through college and kept us from having to really work for a living.

In January, 1977 *TypeWorld* published its first issue. By today's standards, it was pretty amateurish. It was printed on newsprint that began to yellow as it came off the press. The type was ragged right in five columns. And it had 21,000 proofreaders, the initial circulation.

The first issue featured the introduction of the Compugraphic EditWtiter. This was a major announcement at the time as it extended the concept of direct input phototypesetting to include video editing and floppy disk storage. Compugraphic had introduced the first low-cost direct input device, the CompuWriter, in 1971. But it only had a little 32-character display and no storage system.

I know this for a fact since I had been the Marketing Communications Manager at CG (as we called it) and discovered upon arrival there in 1970 that their annual report was set in hot metal type. This was ironic for a company that sold phototypesetters. So I volunteered to set the annual report for 1970 on the CompuWriter. I went in on a Saturday and started typing the copy. After about two hours, I took the cassette to the processor and found that the photo paper had jammed and everything had to be re-input.

There was a crack in the glass of the demo room window after that which no one could explain. It had something to do with the cassette leaving my hands at high velocity. After that I typed one paragraph at a time and processed it. The pasteup was horrendous but Compugraphic got its first phototypeset annual report and I swore I would never again use a device that did not allow re-play of the input. Thus, the EditWriter was destined to be a hot product and the first place anyone read about it was in the first issue of TypeWorld.

Direct input

The CompuWriter was an immediate success. Within two years Compugraphic had four models and a major share of the market. In 1974 Varityper, then a division of Addressograph Multigraph introduced the Comp/Set which added a video display to the output device. It took CG until 1977 to come back with a competitive device.

Press releases

As a Marketing Communications Manager one of my jobs was writing the company's press releases on personnel, new products and more. I had worked in the advertising department of the old Mergenthaler Linotype Company in Brooklyn, NY and moved to New England as Ad Manager for Photon, the company that essentially invented phototypesetting. I left there when the president claimed that the use of the New Testament ("In the beginning, God created the Heavens and the Earth...") as sample text for a type specimen book was "too controversial."

Writing press releases is an interesting exercise. On one hand you have to balance the engineering people who want to emphasize the technical aspects and on the other hand you have the marketing people who have a different agenda. You have to have a quote from someone and then you have to be aware of what the publications might actually print from all that. Too many companies write their press releases like sales brochures, but many are professional and get to the point. And then they get mangled by editors who do not understand what is important.

Phototypesetting was born

Phototypesetting was invented in 1944 by Louis Moyroud and René Higgonet and they brought the technology to the U.S. where it was embraced by a man named Bill Garth and a company called Lithomat. Bill helped to develop it and changed the name of the company to Photon. In 1960 or so he was forced out in a shareholder dispute and he and his chief engineer, Ellis Hansen, formed Compugraphic Corporation. In 1968 they introduced a phototypesetter priced at about $8,000 which then propelled phototypesetting into the mainstream, hastening the death of hot metal and increasing the use of offset lithography.

Phototypesetting was growing like crazy and more and more companies were introducing devices, systems, etc. and there was no single publication that covered this new technology. In the Winter of 1976, Photon, which had been absorbed by Dymo, who made labelmakers, laid off a number of people, one of whom was my former boss from Photon, who had also worked at Linotype. Thus, TypeWorld was started because Sam Blum was out of work.

The idea behind TypeWorld was to reproduce the press releases in more or less their original form so that readers could understand exactly what suppliers were saying and the focus would be on typesetting—and word processing.

In January 1977 TypeWorld appeared in 21,000 mail boxes of printers, publishers, newspapers, prepress services and inplant sites. It was the first time there was one publication that brought all these users together to learn about new technology. There was more than enough material to fill the 28 pages of the first issue. There were ads for paper tape keyboards, video editing systems, converters that changed word processing files into paper tape and even an ad for the Seybold Report, then in its 5th year of publication.

The industry was dominated by Mergenthaler. Harris Intertype had been a major competitor in hot metal but never had the same position in phototype. Photon forced Linotype and Intertype in photo earlier than they would have liked. At first Varityper worked with Photon, but then spun off its own line of equipment. Alphatype had a niche market with typographers and Star Graphic Systems sold to newspapers. MGD, part of Rockwell, has the Metrosetter, a cathode ray tube photosetter, along with Triple-I, who had picked up the RCA (Hell) Videocomp. Itek and Wang were also into typesetting. By 1977, there were over 200 models of phototypesetting machines and word processing devices were evolving into typesetting systems.

There are many parallels to the world of type that was then and the one that is now. The biggest change has been the movement of page creation and production back to the originator, virtually eliminating typesetting services as we knew them. There are still more equipment choices than I think the industry can deal with, now expanded to computer-to-plate and digital color presses which were only dreamed of back then. It is a brave new world.

The Twilight Phone

The answering machine is broken. This is his refrigerator. Please speak very slowly, and I'll stick your message to myself with one of these magnets.

We're sorry. You have reached an imaginary number. You must be an imaginary person.

WE ARE BORG. RESISTANCE IS FUTILE. YOU WILL BE ASSIMILATED. But we're not home right now. So leave a message at the tone, and we'll assimilate you later.

Leave a message. However, you have the right to remain silent. Everything you say will be recorded and used by us.

Hello, this is WBZ, you're on the air.

If you want to leave a message, please wait for the tone. If you want to leave your name and number, please press pound, press 3, then dial your name, then press 6 and dial your number. If you want to leave your name and just a message, press star, press 6, ask for extension 000, then leave your name and message. If you want to leave your number and the time you called, please press star twice, spin in a circle, press 1 twice, talk loud and *beeeep*…

You reached the Sixth Sense Agency. We know who you are and what you want, so at the tone, please hang up.

I can't come to the phone now because alien beings are eating my brain. Leave a message anyway, and after the alien beings assume my shape, one of them will get back to you.

I can't come to the phone because I have amnesia and I feel stupid talking to people I don't remember. Help me out by leaving my name and telling me something about myself.

Heaven, God speaking…

This is a test. This is a test of the Answering Machine Broadcast System. This is only a test.

I AM THE PRESS

Most of the other provisions of the Bill of Rights protect specific liberties or specific rights of individuals. . . . In contrast, the free-press clause extends protection to an institution. The publishing business is, in short, the only organized private business that is given explicit constitutional protection.
—Potter Stewart, Justice of the Supreme Court, 1974

Even Supreme Court Justices can be wrong. It used to be said that freedom of the press belongs to those who own the press. This is not so any more. We are all publishers and we all have a "press."

Lenin said that no one should be allowed to criticize the government and therefore the press should be restricted. In Russia not too long ago you could not even own a copying machine because it was a de facto printing press. Extend that to the printers attached to our computers and most of us have the ability to reproduce and disseminate print at the click of a mouse. Copiers, printers, and presses abound and allow us to multiply pages.

Potter Stewart says publishing is a business and generally that is true. But there is also personal publishing. Years ago in our small town they were going to cut an old elm tree down to make way for a bank parking lot. Kids used copier copies and plastered the town. They got their message to the public. The tree stands to this day.

When the Bill of Rights was enacted the press was not a giant mega-business. It was a group of entrepreneurial individuals, like John Peter Zenger, Ben Franklin and Isaiah Thomas. It was Zenger, not Zenger, Inc. or Time Zenger, whose trial established the bedrock principle of freedom of the press.

The Internet has changed the definition of "press" forever. I have my own Web site. Ergo, I am a publisher. So do millions of other individuals—not companies. It is not always a business; it is a hobby, a cause, or even a whim that motivates them. I compute; therefore I publish.

Freedom of the press is not just for the *New York Times*. It is for anyone with an idea, a principle, or just a big mouth. Freedom of the press is for all of us, because all of us now own the press. We are the PRESS.

More Random Bits

A light year is the distance travelled by light in one year. I think we need a different unit of measurement for typesetting—the light pica—the time it takes light to travel 6 points. Then when someone asks how long it will take to do a job, you can respond "About 20 light picas." Of course, the bold pica is something else entirely.

I don't know why Europeans worry about beef raised with artificial hormones. Just because hamburgers can dance the fandango is no reason not to eat them.

In the *New York Times* computer column, the author stated that you should never buy software at Revision Level 1.0. That means that all suppliers will have to start at Level 2.0 when they introduce new software. NeXT started at .1 and is now at .8 on its way to 1.0 thinking that when they reached 1.0 they would have a stable program. Now they will have to re-think that strategy. Of course, if no one purchased 1.0 of new software, suppliers would never sell anything and could not afford to advertise in newspapers that tell readers not to buy something that is new. Maybe we should start at Level 10.0 and then work backwards so that 1.0 becomes the ultimate version. The article was probably a first draft, level 1.0 if you will. I'll just wait for version 2.0.

Scientists now say that the basic building block of the universe is the quark. There is debate. I say it's a one point em leader dot.

Twenty years ago man walked on the moon for the first time. Plans to condo-ize the Sea of Tranquility have not progressed.

I still remember that Summer night when Armstrong said "The eagle has landed." We woke up our 2-year-old to observe the historic moment. He burped and went back to sleep. Then he went to college and things hadn't changed much in twenty years.

I have not yet begun to procrastinate.

E-mail Boy

In my mind it was only yesterday that I trudged the halls of the old Mergenthaler Linotype Company in Brooklyn, NY delivering the mail to the lowly clerks and the highest officials. As master of the IN and OUT baskets I got to know them, chat a little and function as an integral part of the grapevine, the most effective communication system any organization has. As the entry level job, mail boy provided the opportunity to learn the company and find an eventual niche.

In the early Sixties I stopped at one cubicle and asked the gentleman sitting at an art board what he did. "I correct the errors of my youth," said Hermann Zapf, as he re-did Palatino for the Linofilm.

All this came home to me the other day as I was replying to one of the 70 or so e-mail messages I receive each day. I now have virtual baskets. IN is mail I have not opened; OUT is mail I have replied to. Newsletters appear mysteriously in the e-mail and I read them immediately, while the printed versions now wait a while. Electronic information is almost instantaneous and the only thing faster may be zen publishing.

I still read the print versions and I do not see that habit changing for a long time. But I must admit that I now expect the news to be electronic and the in-depth commentary and technology review to be print.

I guess I am bi-textual.

Think about how we are now located. Your business card and stationery have addresses, both mail and actual location, fax and phone numbers and e-mail addresses, both company and AOL or other. They are all different. Add your Social Security number and all that identifies you.

I subscribe to a digital forum where users and suppliers ask questions, comment, debate or argue about subjects I care about. It is a cyber town hall with a little more time to reflect before making your comments. I read the *Wall Street Journal* on-line (at $69 a year) and there is one less copy printed because of me (sorry). Now there are 300,000 subscribers and that may be 300,000 less copies printed. I read the *New York Times*, the trade press, and other media that have Web sites.

I search the Web like a giant filing cabinet. I deal with artists who send PDFs of art for review. I buy software, flowers and even greeting cards electronically. To paraphrase something Captain Kirk said in one of the Star Trek movies: I live in the world of print but increasingly work in cyberspace.

People send me e-mail telling me to call them or asking if their fax was received. There is an irony in this as we try to balance snail mail, junk mail, fax mail, voice mail, e-mail and perhaps inter-office paper mail. The idea that somehow all that paper could disappear is hard to accept. In the future there may be companies who will decorate your desk with piles of paper instead of plants.

When I travel I routinely plug my Powerbook into a phone jack at a hotel or Amtrak lounge. I am connected, wired, on-line. For years paper piled high on my desk and I fooled myself into thinking I knew where everything was. Now my e-mail is piles of files in a folder and I fool myself into thinking I know where everything is.

Occasionally I print the e-mail and pile it on my desk, which has as much, or more, paper as before. The reason may be nostalgic. The baskets are pretty much gone and so is the mail boy (and later girl). Some companies use robotic carts that travel from office to office and ring a bell for some Pavlovian response as folks rush to the mail cart.

As time goes by there is less and less stuff there and more and more in the computer. Other organizations make you travel to a central mail dropoff or pickup site. All are making e-mail the mandatory tool of communication.

This article was never printed out. It went from my computer to the editor's computer. From there it will be edited on screen and go to the digital page. After a while it will go to film and plate and, by golly, paper. It is truly a brave new world and I miss the little personal notes that folks would send or the comments in the margin of a clipped article.

But now everyone has to type; that is until it becomes v-mail and you use voice. Repetitive stress injury could someday apply to the tongue. Newspapers lost the copy boy. Offices lost the mail boy. The atoms they delivered have gone to bits. E-mail boy is not an option.

The entry level job may now be president.

Multimedia

Multimedia: Watching TV while reading a book listening to the radio and the phone rings. And it's one of those computer calls.

Multimedia lets you see several images on your computer monitor at the same time. My monitor has trouble showing one image and chewing gum at the same time.

Multimedia is an electronic chimera—the head of a TV, the body of a CD-ROM, the soul of a PC, and the mind of MTV.

Multimedia and artificial intelligence are destined for one another. The former certainly causes the latter.

Multimedia manuals are printed. Isn't that a contradiction in terms?

If medium is tedium
Then media are tedia

They say that multimedia gives you virtually unlimited access to information. With it you can learn about almost anything. I felt the same way when I first learned how to use a library.

A multimedia authority once said that someday all workstations will have a key that says "Tell me more." I am very shallow and would prefer a key that says "Tell me less." Or even "Keep it to yourself."

Multimedia is another buzz term. It should just buzz off and go away.

They tell us that we spend almost 5 hours a day watching television at home. Now we spend 8 hours watching computer screens at work. My eyes may retire several years before I do.

Multimedia is more popular in the marketing department than it is in the market. Sort of hype-a-media.

Multimedia really means the integration of video (that is, TV) and computers (that is, computers) to create computer video or digital imaging. This can only lead to computer commercials and digital ads during which I go to the computer restroom or digital john. Eventually the TV and the computer will marry and have Palm Pilots.

Multimedia mania is sweeping the country. Maybe not the whole country. How about Rhode Island? How about Statan Island? How about Fantasy Island?

Multimedia ha! At one event, the informational TV was inoperative and someone affixed a sheet over the screen with the pertinent data. The television was not working; the paper was.

Jack Powers says that 60% of the garbage that goes into landfills is paper. This includes magazines, books and newspapers, read and unread, as well as packaging, junk mail, and assorted odds and ends. This means that there will be multimedia trash too. Instead of filling up landfills, it will fill up our minds.

Me, I'm still monomedia. Or is the monomedium?

Yes, We Have No Bodoni

Type is my life. I learned to kern at my daddy's knee until someone kerned a quoin and his coccyx in one of those wars between east and west or north and south that went with the wind. I made the transition between hot metal linecasting and cold type back in the Sixties. While others were burning draft cards, I melted lead pigs and slung Linotype slugs. You can actually lose an entire decade looking for wrong fonts and widow lines.

I progressed from juggling golf balls on strike-on IBM Composers to punching paper tape for photographic typesetting. I've had glass fonts and plastic fonts and film fonts. I went to digital type with fonts on a floppy. When the technology changed from cathode ray tubes to lasers, I was there. I've seen the good, the bad and the Souvenir.

So when the personal computer came along I was among the first to jump on the bandwagon in the Fall of '81. IBM legitimized the market. Set type with Tandy or Osborne or Kaypro? Give me Big Blue on a desktop any day. It was great to have standardized, off-the-shelf hardware that was readily repairable and upgradable. The software was shrink-wrapped and cheap as type lice. I started with something called Studio Software "Do-it" (which didn't) and Westminster PagePlanner (which also didn't do it). As I went from PC to XT to AT the power beneath my fingers was evident. Keys pulsated and from a distance there was an aura around the monitor. I envisioned an aura around me.

I word processed and spreadsheeted and file managed. Revision 1.0, revision 2.0. Revision, from some language meaning "to squeeze again." Spelling checkers destroyed my ability to spell and on-line thesauri are putting me at a loss for words. With grammar checks and other writing aids, I figure the machine can write the article, edit it, optically read it and then trash it. Automation, what a concept.

I advanced from character printer to dot matrix printer to laser printer with successive A-B and A-B-C boxes to switch from printer to printer to printer (remembering to invoke this utility, that driver, with the right toggle off and don't forget to turn the printer on). More dots, better quality, more fonts, more sizes. I advanced from monochome to color, from EGA to VGA (I think that was the order) and added co-processors, memory boards and other peripherals that plugged into the great computer earth motherboard.

I had serial and parallel cables and plugs with 10 pins and 23 pins. Disk space was always a limitation as I started to add graphics to my text and text to my graphics. I filled floppies from 300K to 1.6MB and then jumped from 10 to 20 to 80MB, with tape backup and removable Bernoullies. Then 1 gigabyte and up to 8 gigs. No matter how much space I had available, I filled it. Data expands to fill the area for its retention. But still I could not see on the screen what my printer would really output. WISWNWIWA: What I Saw Was Not What I Wanted Anyway.

Then came the Macintosh. Finally, a there was machine that dealt with type on screen and off. It actually had menu items for font and size and style. It knew what italic and bold were all about. So what if the screen was small, I could have one for each eyeball or better yet one of those full-sized screens. Naturally I upgraded to the Plus when the time came and bought every revision of every program that put pages together in any way shape or form. I waited in line to buy the Mac II and added more memory, better graphics boards, bigger screens, additional disks, scanners and, of course, PostScript printers.

300dpi advanced to 600dpi and then imagesetters at over 1200dpi. Plain paper, photo paper, film. No more A-B boxes; PostScript was the universal language of printing. I then needed to go from standard pages to tabloid pages, from small printers to big printers. Each new iteration of PostScript called for another RIP. From Redstone to Saturn, 1 to 3 and finally the super high-speed enhanced max turbo RIP that doubles as a microwave oven.

And fonts. I started with 13 and went to the standard 35. There were always new fonts and I bought them by the dozen. The library grew. 50 fonts. 100 fonts. 200 fonts. More disks to store them plus special software to keep track of them. Who needs six versions of Garamond? I do.

Then the programs started to show color and I needed color in hard copy form for proofing. Heck, no one wants to see a black and white proof of a color page or even look at it at on the screen. And I want the color to look like the end product coming off the printing press. That meant special calibration of software and scanner and screen.

More memory, more disks, bigger scanners, more gray levels, more dpi, more fonts, more color, more speed.

So what if I've spent a small fortune over twenty years. So what if there's a pile of stuff in the basement (the V-I-P, a Comp/Edit, a Pacesetter, an Epson FX-80, NEC 3550, PC XT, Xerox 4045, Mac Plus, A-B boxes, old hard disks, an EIT scanner, old monitors, lots of cables, and every revision of every program). I writing this on a 21" 24-bit color Mac Centris 650 with every bell and whistle. And I'm sad. I want the G4 and the kind of power that can send pages back in time. I want the future at my fingertips.

I've got megabytes of memory and gigahertrz of speed
But no matter how much I have there's always more I need

I've got megabytes of ram and mega mips galore
But even with all that I'm still in need of more

My hardware cost keeps climbing, my software cost o my
I guess I'll still be buying until the day I die

And when I reach the pearly gates, it will just be like before.
An infinity of upgrades, an eternity of more.

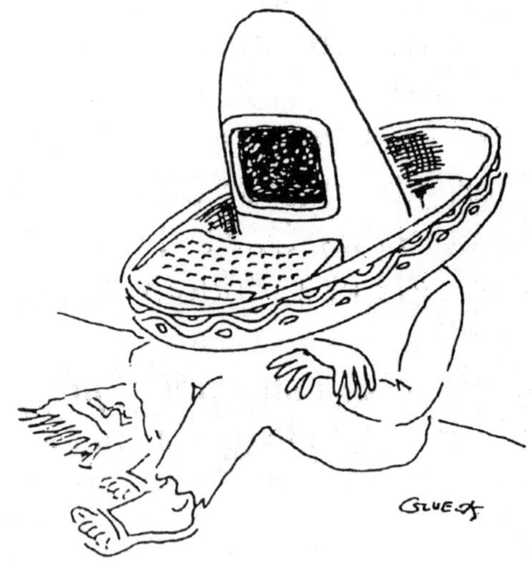

Even More Random Bits

Yeltsin is up to his borscht in problems: ethnic strife, strikes, shortages, unruly politicians. You'd think he was mayor of New York.

The stealth bomber finally left the ground. It had to; it is much too expensive to be a stealth jeep.

The stealth bomber is designed to evade enemy radar. Wouldn't it have been cheaper if it had one of those highway radar detectors used to avoid state troopers on the dashboard?

Radar evasion is not perfected. All the enemy needs is a Massachusetts State Trooper

The president wants to send mankind to Mars. I'd like to just make it through rush hour traffic.

The Exxon Valdez will be converted to a cruise ship and is guaranteed only to leak sun tan oil.

Interesting statistic: the mileage for the Apollo moon mission rocket was five inches per gallon. About the same as my father's 1952 Dodge.

Is it legal to set fire to a Supreme Court Justice in order to express your First Amendment rights? Only if they are wrapped in the flag.

I think my cats are leading a secret life. I have found cat web sites in my bookmarks. And there have been paw prints on the mouse.

Cosmetics companies have stopped testing on animals. It was just inhuman to put false eyelashes and paste-on nails on gerbils to see if they would attract other rodents.

Had an emergency recently so I called the one group that could reach me quickly—Domino's Pizza. They took me to the hospital but we had to make two deliveries en route.

Abort Retry Ignore
Error Messages I Have Known and Loved

Few among us has been fortunate enough to escape the erratic and enigmatic error message. The dirty dozen above will live in infamy, but there are many others lurking just beneath the GUI, some that really tell us what went wrong and some unintelligible to any human being. One Windows NT user swears that they were the victim of this message:

"Can't delete file because there is not enough room on the disk. Delete one or more files."

"Disk not found."
"A Type 1 error has occurred."
"End of file."
"Error -8533."
"Plug-in not found."
"Scratch disk is full."
"Application unknown."
"Out of memory."
"I/O error."
"Document OK but cannot be printed."
"Network is not responding."
"Abort Retry Ignore."

I think it all began when Apple created an error message with a little icon of a bomb that required you to click OK. I wanted the choice "Not OK." Actually, the IBM PC had that wonderful "Abort Retry Ignore" and when you tried the Format command it said "Format Disk - Press any key" and then you tried to abort the function by hitting the Escape key—but that was ANY key and you watched helplessly as the C Drive erased all data.

Old typesetting machines never had error messages; they just did not run. The only error message on your files was the job outputting 72 point type on 10 points of leading for instance. Then you knew something went wrong. The object of modern error messages is to tell the what and why of problems.

Some error messages are as provocative as the Delphic Oracle of ancient history. If you asked "Will I be king?" it might reply "You will be crowned." Today it would reply "Invalid input."

I was able to locate the people who write computer error messages. At first I thought they might be the people who edit lengthy video recordings into out-of-context sound bites—not sound bytes. It turns out that their pithy prose had formerly been entombed inside fortune cookies and this experience was well suited to the also ambiguous and obtuse computer error message.

At present they are tied up on Y2K error messages, like "Not a valid century" and "O O NO NO."

We found a collection of real and imagined error messages on the Web. Here are some of our favorites:

Error 13: Illegal brain function. Process terminated.
REALITY.SYS corrupted—Unable to recover Universe
USER ERROR: Replace user and press any key to continue.
Volume in Drive C: TOO_LOUD!
Press [ESC] to detonate or any other key to explode.
BREAKFAST.COM halted—cereal port not responding.
Virus detected! P)our chicken soup on motherboard?
File not found! Reformat hard drive? [YN]
Spellchecker not found. Press -- to continue.
A)bort, R)etry or S)elf-destruct?
A)bort, R)etry, I)gnore, V)alium?
A)bort, R)etry, I)nfluence with large hammer.
A)bort, R)etry, P)ee in disk drive.
Backup not found: A)bort, R)etry, M)assive heart failure?
Bad command or file name. Go stand in the corner.
Close your eyes and click your mouse three times.
DYNAMIC LINK ERROR: Your mistake is now everywhere.
SENILE.COM found. Out Of Memory.
APATHY ERROR: Don't bother striking any key.
Error 52: Whatever.
Type 11 error. Unsure but who cares?
Type 11 Error. That's two Type1s.

I have always wondered about that message that says "PostScript error. File is OK but cannot be output." In one respect, computers are just like us: they have no idea what is going on. Here are some suggestions for error messages for the new millennium:

"System error. Deep doo doo ahead."
"Error -1111. We have no idea either."
"Something bad is about to happen. Run."
"This document cannot be printed. Ever."
"A giant asterisk is about to impact the earth and destroy life as we know it. Press any key."
"Application has unexpectedly quit. If it had been expected you could have planned for it."
"Something bad has happened which has no error message."
"Don't know. Don't care."
"Panic."
"Abort, Retry, Ignore, Fail?"
"This document is aesthetically displeasing and has been erased."
"You should have bought a Mac."
"Your prayer was unable to make a socket connection. God may not be accepting connections at this time."

To avoid the conflicts that plague us all, I acquired a program that listed all error messages with an explanation for each. My first use was greeted with "File is OK but cannot be opened." Then I tried one of those conflict catchers. It would not open because it conflicted with one of the weird Word extensions.I even get an error message when I turn the computer on: "This computer was not shut down properly." I guess shutdown procedures must be as formal as a Japanese Tea Ceremony.

Recently I was at a Chinese restaurant and crumbled the fortune cookie to reveal the message, perhaps this time the ultimate truth, the meaning of life.

It said:

"Help. I'm being held prisoner inside a computer factory."

After a recent article on the strange side of computer use, readers sent me their experiences in this area.

Tech: What's the problem?
User: There is smoke coming out of the power supply.
Tech: You'll need a new power supply.
User: No, I don't! I just need to change the startup files.
Tech: Sir, the power supply is faulty. You need to replace it.
User: No way! Someone told me that I just needed to change the startup files and it will fix the problem! All I need is for you to tell me the command.

The unlucky 13 tech support replies

1. Strange . . .
2. Never heard about that.
3. It did work yesterday.
4. The machine seems to be broken.
5. Has the operating system been updated?
6. Yes yes, it will be ready in time.
7. Oh, it's just a feature.
8. Of course, I just have to do these small fixes.
9. It will be done in no time at all.
10. It's just some unlucky coincidence.
11. It's already there, but it has not been tested.
12. It works, but it's not been tested.
13. There must be a virus in the application software.

A caller explained they had received a gift of software on 5.25-inch diskettes, but they had only a 3.5-inch disk drive. The technician said they could get a second disk drive, or use 3.5-inch diskettes. The customer called back later, now complaining that the disk drive was making a terrible noise. The technician determined the caller had used a pair of scissors to trim the 5.25-inch diskettes to fit the 3.5-inch drive.

The computer was doing nothing. No problem, the technician said. First, open a window to launch a specific program. The caller asked a few moments later if it might be all right to close the window. because it was getting chilly.

I saw someone putting a credit card into a floppy drive and pulling it out very quickly. I inquired as to what they were doing and they said they were shopping on the internet, and they were asked for a credit card number, so they were using the ATM "thingy."

Perpetual power

I worked with an individual who plugged their power strip back into itself and could not understand why their computer would not turn on.

A fax-pas

1st Person: "Do you know about this fax machine?"
2nd Person: "A little. What's wrong?"
1st Person: "Well, I sent a fax, and the recipient called back to say all she received was a cover sheet and a blank page. I tried it again, and the same thing happened."
2nd Person: "How did you load the sheet?"
1st Person: "It's a pretty sensitive memo, and I didn't want anyone else to read it by accident, so I folded it so only the recipient would open it and read it."

Ready, Set, No Go

Tech Support: "What does the screen say now."
Person: "It says, "Hit ENTER when ready."
Tech Support: "Well?"
Person: "How do I know when it's ready?"

An intern was typing and turned to a secretary and said, "I'm almost out of typing paper. What do I do?" "Just use copier machine paper," the secretary told them. With that, the intern took the last remaining blank piece of paper, put it on the photocopier and proceeded to make five blank copies.

One of our servers crashed. I was watching our new system administrator trying to restore it. He inserted a CD and needed to type a path name to a directory named "i386." He started to type it and paused, asking me "Where's the key for that line thing?" I asked what he was talking about, and he said, "You know, that one that looks like an upside-down exclamation mark." I replied, "You mean the letter 'i'?" and he said, "Yeah, that's it!"

I was in a car dealership a while ago when a large new motor home was towed into the garage. The front of the vehicle was in dire need of repair. I asked the manager what had happened. He told me that the driver had set the cruise control, then went in the back to use the computer.

Lastly, my favorite tech support conversation:

Q: My Etch-A-Sketch has a distorted display. What should I do?
A: Pick it up and shake it.

Q: How do I boot my Etch-A-Sketch?
A: Pick it up and shake it.

Q: My Etch-A-Sketch has these funny little lines all over the screen.
A: Pick it up and shake it.

Q: How do I turn my Etch-A-Sketch off?
A: Pick it up and shake it. Set it down.

Q: How do I delete a document from my Etch-A-Sketch?
A: Pick it up and shake it.

Q: How do I keep from losing my Etch-A-Sketch document?
A: Stop shaking it.

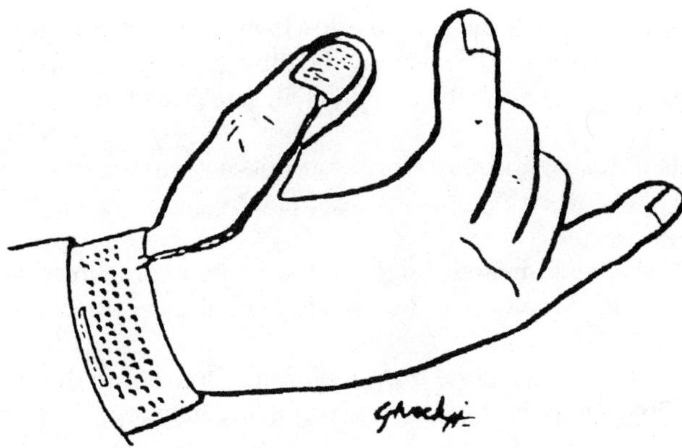

Mankind Does Not Live by Mouse Alone

Steve Jobs once said that machines can accelerate human power. He said that the computer is a bicycle for our minds. Sme of us need training wheels.

I would have been here earlier but my knowledge navigator broke down and I had to fly by the seat of my computer. I put the mouse on manual override.

I saw a book called "OS2 Illustrated." The pages were all blank.

Just bought "The Complete Idiot's Guide to Dummies" or was it "The Complete Dummy's Guide to Idiots"?

These books sell very well. And every purchaser is an admitted idiot or dummy. I'm a recovering typographer myself.

For those of you who are really weird, there is now an inflatable Macintosh. You blow it up through the SCSI tube.

Gauguin said that he shut his eyes in order to see. He had a braille GUI.

One of the impressionist artists said "With an apple I will take Paris." With a PC I will take Cleveland.

Just think: it is now possible to create Century Expanded Condensed Bold Outline Drop Shadow Oblique Small Caps Superscript. And then someone will say "Match it."

Our industry and our world are not at a crossroad—they are at a cloverleaf. Or is it a dead end?

Fat free, sodium free, sugar free—do you sometimes feel that some people should be labeled "intelligence free."

Computers have gone from mainframe to mini to desktop to laptop to palmtop. Coming soon: fingertip top.

Computers are useless without us. Prove it for yourself: go up to the machine and tell it to make a page. Without you nothing happens. So the real question is: which one of us is the tool?

The very notion of an electronic brain is ludicrous. At my age an electronic kidney would be better.

Computers follow instructions exactly. In this respect they are totally unlike teenagers.

The Library of Congress is one of the largest repositories of human knowledge in the world. So close to Congress yet so far away.

Congress now gets the Congressional Record online so they can not read it sooner.

We have now become electronic voyeurs, as we surf the Internet, peering into files on the data highway.

C code.
C code run.
C code bomb.
C code sad.
C code in therapy.

My motto: Procrastinate now!

Someday, when there is time travel, you will be able to put things off until yesterday.

And then it will be precrastination.

Cogito eggo sum. I think, therefore I waffle.

Descartes really said: I think, therefore I RAM.

V RAM would have been more.

Que sera serif. What will be, will be roman.

Be Different, Conform

During the Renaissance one person could possess the sum total of human knowledge. Today, only teenagers have that ability.

There are no acronyms in the Chinese language. Now, who really has the higher civilization?

A short history of the world
Once there were dinosaurs and no computers.
Now there are computers and no dinosaurs.
The end

Desktop publishing, desktop prepress...and now—Desktop Desktop—the ultimate buzzterm. It can mean anything. Add a modifier and it becomes Digital Desktop Desktop, which is different from Digital Digital or Desktop Digital Digital.

Just think, space satellites let us transmit poor quality around the world.

Art and skill: we can automate skill, but Heaven help us when we automate art.

I operate my microwave by microwave and my remote control by remote control. And you wonder why I'm out of touch.

A friend of mine has a really cheap PC—it only does the work of ten bureaucrats.

I think I know why Microsoft and Apple want to get into fonts: revisions. As in Helvetica 1.0, Helvetica 1.2, Helvetica 2.0.

Well, both sons are now gainfully employed and I await the day they say "Dad, you've supported us, now it's our turn to take care of you and mom."

Oat bran does destroy your mind.

The Bionic Color

Now it can be revealed. Uncovered military files reveal a super secret weapon-of-mass-destruction development program, code-named Project Hoboken (changed from Project Mosaic because the name was taken), that formulated a color so lethal it could destroy any observer, even those with 20/50 eyesight. Tints as low as 5% of the color caused serious injury and sunglasses provided no protection.

This color was an outgrowth of a research program to develop stealth hues for camouflage purposes. The resulting killer color was tested on bacteria in a remote unpopulated area—the Marv Albert Fan Club—on a fateful day when visibility was limited. It was feared that the color might be reflected towards civilian populations. The results were devastating. One scientist muttered "To be or RGB, now we have become the rainbow of my discontent." Not all scientists make sense.

Special bombs containing colored dyes were constructed. Inter-continental ballistic fireworks were developed. Military personnel were given sealed envelopes containing swatches of the color instead of handguns. These were printed by color blind printers in a darkened, hermetically sealed plant. An anti-color missile project tried for years to find a Star Wars defense against incoming colors. Scientists from the original project petitioned the president to never use such an inhuman weapon. "Let us seek peaceful uses for color," they implored. "We can harness the awesome power of CMYK to create a better world."

There was one time when cold fusion color looked hopeful, but no color reactor has ever been built. Several years ago a printer in Keokuk, Iowa inadvertently created the horrific hue while trying to satisfy an art director who wanted "just a shade lighter, but not too light."

Both were in therapy for many years and refuse to discuss the incident. The plant was secretly dismantled and stored at the national toxic waste storage area but there is a fear that the color could contaminate the nuclear waste. The terrifying tint was assigned an unlisted Pantone number and filed away forever. The government disavows any knowledge of the bionic color.

Y2K2

E-mail to God@galactic.com

I tried to reach you through dial-a-prayer.org but I got a 404 error. You must get a lot of spam. As You know, I don't ask for much. Well, there was that time the 707 tried to land on the 87th floor of the Sears Tower. Please excuse the yelling.

Here is my simple request—do I have to phrase it in the form of a prayer? Can we get all the software suppliers on earth (although some may not be from this planet) to not introduce anything new for one year? That's right—not introduce anything for one year.

No revisions. No upgrades. No changes. My vote is for the palindromic year of 2002—Y2K2. There is only one of these every century, like 1881, 1991, 2002, and 2112, so we have a window of opportunity coming up. I would call it the year of computer peace, or pax computus.

You see, the I had to upgrade my Mac to OS 8.5 in order to run Adobe InDesign. Usually, when it comes to operating systems, I wait a year until everyone stops complaining, but I had no choice. As soon as I loaded 8.5, I discovered that I needed 8.51. I found it on the Apple web site and downloaded it. Done. I like being able to get upgrades that fast. But then some of my control panel programs bombed the machine. I think bad breath bombed the machine.

I bought Norton Disk Doctor but I think I really need a Norton Disk Doctor. No, Disk Psychiatrist.

I also bought one of those crash protection programs, which I believe protects the crash, not the system. Thus, it tells me when I am going to crash instead of just crashing like it did before. If it gave me some clue or even a week's notice, that would be better. Plus, whenever I copy to or from a Zip disk, the system hangs. I am zippless. So I went to OS 8.6 and that fixed some things, but now other things go wrong. And OS7 is imminent.

Upgrades and revisions are wearing me down. I just realized that the Ten Commandments are still at Revision 1.0—have You thought about a Dummy's Guide? Or, how about Rev 1.1 and you add a few more commandments about people who wear nose rings or anything on the Fox network.

Everything was running fine with OS 8. I was happy. But then I was happy with OS 7 as well. Although I now remember the problems going from 7.5 to 8. Eventually I will have to go to Acrobat 4, Photoshop 5, Illustrator 8, and QuarkXPress 4.4, plus upgrades to ATM, Suitcase, printer drivers, and more.

The computers keep changing to get more power to run the new operating systems to support the applications programs which keep getting bigger to do more things and require more power from the OS and more speed and memory and storage from the hardware. There is no end to it and I'm getting too old for this. I had hair when the desktop revolution started.

Did You have the same problem going from Adam to Eve? It was a model change, right?

I know there is a future Acrobat 5, Photoshop 6, Illustrator 9, QuarkXPress 5, and even an InDesign 2, even though we haven't even gotten to 1. But at some point, we have to take a rest. How many new features can I handle? Many programs look like the cockpit of a Boeing 777.

But I'm not being petty, God. After almost 20 years of PC and Mac upgrades, I should be used to it. I remember going from the Kaypro to the XT in 1981 and from the original Mac to the Fat Mac in 1985. I must have spent 15% of my life doing upgrades and revisions and trying to figure out why something that did work now no longer works. It has been maddening. That's when it finally hit me: don't we all deserve one year of peace? Just one year. All programs, OSes, inits, etc. run without incident. From January 1, 2002 to December 31, 2002 every supplier shrink wraps their development group.

By then OS X will be introduced for the Mac and I don't even want to hear about OS XI—it sounds like the Super Bowl. How about OS X.5, a unique blend of roman and arabic numerals. There might even be an OS MCMXXI eventually. Windows 2000 is also on the horizon and You may want to increase the availability of Prozac.

I would even pay a little bit more for every program just for a vacation from the trials and tribulations of upgrades ...for just 12 months, one year. Please understand, God, I am not a luddite. I like technology. It has made me more productive. The computer has cut my work in half. That's why I bought two of them.

But every time I upgrade or revise, there is some set of occurrences that require me to fix something. To fix it, I have to figure out what the problem is and that is the real problem. All of a sudden, something that worked stops working. Why? Who knows? Okay, You know but you don't tell me. I have to track the problem down and all this takes time. And of course it is the worst possible time to happen.

And, if You can get one year of peace out of the computer industry, God, You certainly can get the world to cool it for one year. We could have peace between the Indians and the Pakistanis, the Serbs and the Albanians, and even the Republicans and the Democrats. We could then take all that money we spend on bullets and bombs and guns and save it up for a really good purpose:

The upgrades that will be coming in 2003. Amen.

Information Overload

It is the electronic world of pure information behind your computer screen. You don't go through the looking glass; you are the looking glass.

Data: 0=off, 1=on.
Information: Binary 10=2.
Knowledge: It takes 2 to tango.
Wisdom: It is better to dance with girls than squid.

Fuzzy logic may be the gray area between yes and no.

Just read Alvin Toffler's new book called "Powershift" (he was the author of "Future Shock") in which he states that money is power and knowledge is power and power is power. Nothing like making up your mind. The real power may be knowing what power is.

He claims that some day money will be programmable. Instead of recessions, we will have a monetary virus.

Can you imagine currency revisions? Inflation?.

He says that the worldwide exports of intellectual property are now equal to food, fuel and manufactured goods. Whenever I hear "intellectual property," I can only think of William F. Buckley's summer home.

Pseudo-intellectual property would be fantasy land. If it needs a lot of work, it would be a taxing shelter.

I would have been here earlier but my knowledge navigator broke down and I had to fly by the seat of my CPU.

We needed more data for decision making so they told us computers were the answer. The computers generated more data than we could deal with so they told us that hypertext and intelligent databases would help us find information faster. So now we have to use the computer to find the information because the computer creates more information than we actually need.

The amount of data that we must deal with daily is increasing rapidly. We are becoming informaniacs.

Informania: what a concept.

You realize that information is growing at such a rapid rate that we cannot absorb it. I'm working on data pills that will allow you to take information orally. For kids, they will look like Flintstone characters and for adults they will resemble Quaaludes. The bottle has the warning "Do not exceed dosage or you will be too smart for your own good."

DVD-ROM can store gigabytes of data. The Paperwork Reduction Act is meaningless. We need a Data Reduction Act.

Knowledge is power. But invest in oil.

At the beginning of the French Revolution they tore down the Bastille. At the start of the Information Revolution I tore up a rather vicious memo.

"There is a difference" department. Information tells you that the pot is hot. Knowledge tells you not to touch it. Experience reminds you not to touch it.

I don't need more information. At my age, I can't remember the old information.

Information is transitory
Knowledge endures
Computers do not create
They are only messengers

I'm having an information overload, so shut up.

There is a worldwide information glut. We ought to raise the price to cut demand.

Information in the move: informotion.

Some people want to be information navigators. I want to be an information bombardier.

BOOK

You may have read this before, but I like it, so here it is:

Introducing the new Bio-Optic Organized Knowledge device, trade named BOOK. BOOK is a revolutionary breakthrough in technology: no wires, no electric circuits, no batteries, nothing to be connected or switched on. It's so easy to use, even a child can operate it.

Compact and portable, it can be used anywhere -- even sitting in an armchair by the fire -- yet it is powerful enough to hold as much information as a CD-ROM disc. Here's how it works:

BOOK is constructed of sequentially numbered sheets of paper (recyclable), each capable of holding thousands of bits of information.

The pages are locked together with a custom-fit device called a binder which keeps the sheets in their correct sequence. Opaque Paper Technology (OPT) allows manufacturers to use both sides of the sheet, doubling the information density and cutting costs. Experts are divided on the prospects for further increases in information density; for now, BOOKS with more information simply use more pages.

Each sheet is scanned optically, registering information directly into your brain. A flick of the finger takes you to the next sheet.

BOOK may be taken up at any time and used merely by opening it.

BOOK never crashes or requires rebooting, though like other display devices it can become unusable if dropped overboard. The "browse" feature allows you to move instantly to any sheet, and move forward or backward as you wish. Many come with an "index" feature, which pinpoints the exact location of any selected information for instant retrieval.

An optional "BOOKmark" accessory allows you to open BOOK to the exact place you left it in a previous session--even if the BOOK has been closed. BOOKmarks fit universal design standards; thus, a single BOOKmark can be used in BOOKs by various manufacturers.

Conversely, numerous BOOK markers can be used in a single BOOK if the user wants to store numerous views at once. The number is limited only by the number of pages in the BOOK.

You can also make personal notes next to BOOK text entries with an optional programming tool, the Portable Erasable Nib Cryptic Intercommunication Language Stylus (PENCILS).

Portable, durable, and affordable, BOOK is being hailed as a precursor of a new entertainment wave. Also, BOOK's appeal seems so certain that thousands of content creators have committed to the platform and investors are reportedly flocking. Look for a flood of new titles soon.

Not Even God and Rutherford B. Hayes Are Spared from Junk Mail

If you're looking for God, Sumter County, Florida, might be a good place to start. At least that's what the folks at American Family Publishers seem to think.

The company earlier this year mailed a sweepstakes notice addressed to "God" to a church in Bushnell, about 60 miles north of Tampa. The message: "God" is a finalist for the $11 million top prize.

"God, we've been searching for you," American Family wrote in the letter received by the Bushnell Assembly of God. If God were to win, the letter stated, "What an incredible fortune there would be for God!" according to the Sumter County Times, which first reported the divine mix-up. "Could you imagine the looks you'd get from your neighbors? But don't just sit there, God."

Church pastor Bill Brack said, "I always thought He lived here, but I didn't actually know." The pastor is considering mailing in the entry; his 140-person congregation could use the money. "I'm willing for them to show up here at the church with cameras and me in my bathrobe as long as they write a check." [To God?] And what would happen if a different winner were chosen? "God would be disappointed," Brack said.

Ambitious Florida travel agents went right to the top and asked a former U.S. president to buy a Caribbean vacation—but they picked one who has been dead 105 years. "Dear Rutherford, We're excited for you," said the direct mail postcard addressed to Rutherford B. Hayes. The card arrived at the Rutherford B. Hayes Presidential Center in Fremont, Ohio, and offered a rental car, round-trip Caribbean cruise and Florida hotel accommodation. The offer was declined. "Rutherford's a little lethargic these days," presidential center spokeswoman Nancy Kleinhenz told the newspaper. The card was sent by the Florida Travel Network. The marketing director said someone at the presidential center might have used the institution's name to buy a mail-order item, resulting in the center being added to a direct- mail marketing list, adding that it was up to recipients to ask that they be removed from direct mail lists.

Paper Tigers

I like paper. It may be a one dimensional medium in a multi-media world, but it is friendly and portable. I like paper. Then someone countered "What if the paper could talk?" Wow. If I tore it would it cry? If it talked too much could I shut it up with scotch tape? Would a ream be noisy?

Would tinted paper have an accent and heavy stocks talk with a deep voice? If paper talks, would other stationery items get jealous? Would paper clips form a heavy metal band? I can visualize someone returning some paper because it was reticent: "This is a bad batch; it mumbles."

Paper is not dead and is not dying. It just isn't sexy. It does not sing and dance.

We may reduce it on one end but it comes back on the other.

Only now the customer pays for the paper.

Reading on a screen is okay, but books will exist for three reasons: bed, bath and beach.

After using a computer, when you are reading a real book, do you look for the mouse to get to the next page?

When you get in the elevator do you double-press the button for the floor you want?

Just before I go to sleep, I think "shutdown."

But we do waste paper. 30% of all that is printed is thrown away unread.

There will be a paperless office when there are no more offices. The ultimate in downsizing. Downsizing is like reverse Viagra. We will all work at home.

I can say without fear of contradiction: paper does not have viruses and will not crash in Y2K.

Today's offices run on paper. It is a cultural thing. Think of all the people who carry a sheet of paper around. Take away paper and you are doomed to stay in your cubicle. Paper gives you a reason to get out.

I'm taking this down to the print shop. The print shop is always down.

Third sub basement, left at the dumpster. The computer department is always up. There's a sign on the interstate: this exit to computer center.

Paper is democratic. It does not discriminate because of age, sex, race, creed, or economic level.

It is user friendly. By the way, user friendly bills?

Dear Frank: How are you? You know, you owe us a few bucks. How do you feel about that?

Paper lasts longer than recorded media. I have seen the Dead Sea Scrolls.

If they were the Dead CD-ROMs, forget it.

Try to find a Syquest 44mb drive in your company. Play that video of your wedding on your 20th anniversary if you can find a VHS player. And if you went Beta . . .

And stop telling me that we kill trees. We also kill wheat. I don't see anyone chaining themself to a corn stalk.

If fact we will be using kenaph and hemp to make pulp.

Print is digital. Whether you make a plate offline or on the press with ink or you use toner or inkjet, we take digital files and output spots, dots and pixels. We will replicate information on paper with presses, printers, copiers and mopiers.

Print and paper are only one way of communicating or publishing. Can't we just get along?

But most of print is static. Every image off the press is the same. If they were different, something is wrong. We see dynamic printing as an advantage.

Dynamic printing enables

Personalization
Tie it to your database and you have a whole new way of communicating, selling, relating.

Publications on demand
Books that are never out of print. Although some deserve to go away, like all those published about OJ Simpson.

We have always had on demand printing. You go to the printer and demand your printing.

Immediacy
We live in the ex FedEx age. I can't wait until tomorrow. I absolutely, positively want it now. Went into Minuteman Press. Print this, I said. Come back in three days, he said. Then change your sign, I said.

Distribute and print
We can move bits faster than we can move trucks of paper.

Re-purposability
Spots on paper to pixels on screen and back again.

It really comes down to workflow. I like the systems that use barcodes to keep track of job components. Someday barcodes may be tattooed on babies when they are born and there will be sensors on every corner.

Where's Johnny? 5th and Main. That would help finding your way when you are lost. Strategically positioned signs could say "Hey Frank, turn left."

We all need to learn new tricks. For years we have been at the mercy of the printers. Now we are at the mercy of the geeks. Managing geeks is like herding cats.

It all comes down to managing your intellectual property. Intellectual property is what universities are built on.

When I think of a data warehouse I imagine a tiny forklift,

E-commerce, e-business. I browsed on over to the e-mall and made a purchase using cybercash. It got ripped off. I was e-mugged. And someone dented my computer in the parking lot.

The new world is—document the program and program the document.

Someday, genetic engineering may create people who are documents. E-genes may even be in our future.

The longer I live, the less future there is to worry about.

I do know that technology does not always solve problems. My father was once replaced with a gadget that did everything he did, only better. The sad thing is that my mother bought one.

We want everything to be easy. How about a book called "Easy UNIX?"

How about the Dummies guides. We want Cliff Notes for Cliff Notes. They have Dummies books for wine and gardening and even sex education. It's a pop up book.

Pictures lie—sure, they learned it from words.

Romano's Law: references to Moore's Law increase with each succeeding speaker.

The definition of obsolete: any computer you own.

My computer is apathetic: Don't bother striking any key, it tells me.

Who is making money in printing and publishing, besides counterfeiters?

A Problem for Every Solution

Typesetters lost their work to their customers. Prepress services are losing it to printers. Printers are losing it to electronic publishers. All because we went desktop.

Almost all of the desktop products are under $1,000, sold through dealers and VARs and direct mail. Additional revenue comes from revisions—revision, from the Latin "revise"—to squeeze again.

All programs are now moving to all platforms to offer capability to any user of any workstation. Mac programs are going to Windows, Windows programs are going to Mac. UNIX programs are going to LINUX. CP/M may actually be back.

Desktop programs started with big systems and then went to desktop on virtually every platform and they are now talking about customized systems. They may now have a problem for every solution.

This market was most affected by desktop programs. Many users put in networks of PCs and Macs with inexpensive programs and created their own systems. We traded bigger systems at big dollars for smaller systems at small dollars.

Art and design markets are important. There are 900,000 art professionals in the U.S. Some of them have trouble with Magic Markers; imagine their use of a mouse. We should make it in the shape of an X-Acto.

International sales are vital. Over half of all revenue is now derived from the rest of the world. Actually 47% of our industry is owned by the rest of the world.

Desktop changed the way we market. Instead of a sales person trying to find the customer for the product, the customer tries to find the product and the sales person.

People look at this stuff and say "That's crap. How much is the machine?" "$400." "That's not bad crap."

Many of you are moving into color. EFI just tried to copyright the color orange. If the first years of desktop publishing produced *near quality* printout we can expect the first years of color publishing to produce *near sighted* color.

Remember the CompuWriters and EditWriters and Linocomps and Linoterms and Comp/Sets and Comp/Edits and others. Those of you who operated them will be very comfortable with HTML. They made up 80% of all the typesetters sold. If we do not control the low end part of the market, we are not planting the seeds that allow us to go back and sell upgrades, new systems, etc. We are losing the low end to plain paper imagesetters in the 600dpi and above range.

When desktop publishing came along almost every artist started to do what others used to do for them. The same folks who returned galleys for a two-letter kern now do their own type, do their own kerning, do their own scanning, and do their own trapping. They only thing they don't do is do it right. They design things we can't print, but if we don't print it makes no difference. We are united by technology; we are separated by technology.

Remember the rallying cry of the desktop a decade ago: "No codes!" We were told about "user friendly" I remembered that the other day as I keyed Command-Option-Control-Shift-Letter-Left Elbow-Leg-Up-Jump-Down-Spin-Around-Pick-a-Bale-of-Cotton-F8-Escape. The Kama Sutra but without the eroticism.

The controls in Microsoft Word look like the cockpit of a 747. I need a co-pilot. It comes with a black box. The other day the system crashed and they recovered the box—operator error.

User Unfriendly

- Word processing programs replace a typewriter and White-Out with a $600 program with 200 commands that let you concentrate on writing.
- File management programs replace index cards with a $600 program with 200 commands to let you concentrate on data management.
- Graphics programs replace pen and ruler with a $600 program with 200 commands to let you concentrate on drawing and painting.
- Spreadsheets replace calculators and graph paper with a $600 program with 200 commands to let you concentrate on calculations.
- Publishing programs replace typesetting and pasteup with a $600 program with 300 commands that let you concentrate on documents.

The result is $3,000 in software with over 1,000 commands. Each program is easy, in and of itself, but the cumulative result may kill me. *They all have one thing in common: they're different and the cumulative result is overwhelming. Just think of the number of keyboard shortcuts to remember.*

I tried to buy a 14" tray for my laser printer. The dealer was not interested in the order. So I went elsewhere and ordered a laser printer and a 14" tray...and told them to cross off the printer. Try to buy high-density floppies at CompUSA. They give you a catalog and an 800 number.

I was word processing with a screen saver active and a memory enhancer installed, and when I keyed option shift tab the toasters came on and the system crashed with the message: "Something bad has happened and we have no idea what."

I called the 800 number and the phone picked up on the third ring. The message:

If you have a PC with DOS, key 1, a PC with Windows, key 95, a Powerbook 5300, key 3 and stand back from the phone, any other computer, key the Lord's Prayer.

If you are an atheist, key 1, an agnostic, key 2, an unaffiliated deist, key 3.

If you are a registered user, key 1, an unregistered user, key 2, a scumsucking violator of intellectual property, key 3.

If you're for abortion, key 1, anti abortion, key 2, already been aborted, key 3.

If you are a programmer go to 1, a typographer, shift to 2, a printer, press 3.

The phone rings and a machine comes on "All of our lines are busy, please call back." When you finally get to a human being they say "We never heard of that problem. Try reloading your software" I would love to be a plumber when one of those phone tech reps calls for service. They say "My toilet is backed up and it's flooding the house" and I say "Never heard of that problem. Try re-piping your house."

You want a computer, call a retail store.
You want a scanner, call a dealer.
You want a printer, call a tele-marketer.
You want software, call an 800 number.
You want service and support, call 911.

Eventually you will order an imagesetter by dialing a 900 number and $27,000 will be added to your phone bill. And you won't even get heavy breathing.

But it is never one battle that determines victory. It is the total campaign from the opening shot to the final sales report. Marketing is war. You don't want to be the poor dumb bastard to lose the order for your company, you want the other poor dumb bastard to lose the order for their company. Enough of this war analogy, I wouldn't want to be attacked by a militant peace activist.

If we do not generate profits, if we do not make money, we will all lose. R&D will be reduced. Consolidations will create giant conglomerates that could exert adverse pressures. Like "1984" we could mistake slogans for solutions.

I like the competition of free enterprise. I like order and stability. Life is not that simple. Like the confusion I experienced when I shipped my FAX machine by Federal Express.

Customers know that there will be new things, so they stop buying the old things. And yet the old things work. We are creating emotional obsolescence. What you have works, but you feel bad because there is a newer version. I believe the best time to buy anything is last year.

When I was young I saw an ad in a DC comic book for a walkie talkie. It was $1 and advertised no batteries and no electricity. I saved up the buck and set it in. A few weeks later came two plastic cups and about six feet of string. Ever since then, I have felt that technology promises much but does not always deliver. Technology cannot overcome the lack of ability, or human resources.

But now a word from our sponsor

The industry I grew up in is having an identity crisis. What market are we in? Remember when we switched from hot metal to phototypesetting? Then to computer typesetting. And then to video editing and multi-terminal systems. Then to CRT typesetting and then to laser imaging. It was all so definable. It was typesetting or printing, commercial or corporate. Then sometime in the Eighties it became publishing.

Now I hear or new markets. Multimedia is said to be a half trillion dollar market . . . plus or minus half a trillion dollars. No one can define multimedia which is why the market is so big.

Business Week described a $93 billion document publishing market...which is greater than the total value of shipments of the entire commercial printing industry, at just under $90 billion. The difference must be postage and handling.

A decade ago the market for electronic corporate publishing was estimated at $52 billion. It was off by $50 billion. Military programs were cut and the documentation that went with them. The Pentagon is now establishing standards for stealth documentation. Remember the tech doc systems of the early Eighties: Texet, Omnipage, Bedford, Demonics, Royce, Xyvision, and others. Where do these inflated projections come from?

Here's how it works: someone gets up at an event like this and creates a new buzzword. "The market for tapioca publishing is huge," says so and so. So and so will work for two or three vendors at higher and higher levels of incompetence and then disappear, winding up as a shoe salesman in Keokuk. The press picks up the quote and finds another person to support it. "Yep, tapioca publishing is big. I see it as a billion dollar market," says consultant such and such.

A research publisher jumps on the buzzwagon and issues a report claiming a *multi* billion market. Other researchers cannot be left in the lurch and issue their reports, each claiming bigger and bigger markets to show that they really know about tapioca publishing.

New companies come into existence and small groups split away from established firms. Venture capitalists give them money; venture capitalists force money upon them. Newsletters are promoted with the inside dope, written by same. Seminar sessions are developed and a new conference is presented. One by one, every supplier announces their commitment to tapioca publishing, even if they don't know what it is. The press does special sections and columnists proclaim "It's the super app of the Nineties."

A magazine is created to cover the new market and then a trade show: TapiocaWorld. Later, projections say the technology isn't ready, the users aren't ready, the market isn't ready. Tapioca publishing becomes a footnote to history. In the meantime, the consultants, researchers, publishers, show promoters and investment advisors have made a fortune. They were right, tapioca publishing was a billion dollar market.

Getting back: Imagesetters produce film and imposetters produce imposed film. Computer to plate eliminates film because film is bad. Film makers eliminate silver and chemistry and film is good again. Laser printers eliminate film and plates. Digital color printers eliminate film, plates and printing presses. Electronic publishing eliminates film, plates, printers, presses and paper. Markets without consumables are not often very large markets. It may be that personal computers, their software and most peripherals are the new consumables.

Prepress, or printing foreplay, is about $5 billion depending on how well Agfa is doing this month. The health of the printing industry really depends on the value of the yen, the mark, the shekl, the Euro and Alan Greenspan's personal life. It is worldwide.

Desktop publishing depends on how you define it. If you count every laser printer the market is enormous. If you only count laser printers used by people who don't call the font Hel-a-va-tika, it's not that big.

Fonts are a big business…if you introduce a new format. You could wake up one day and find Truetype, Truetype GX, PostScript Type 1, Type 1 Multiple Masters, Type 1 GX and Type 1 Multiple Masters GX fonts in you system. This calls for more than a font reunion. You can control both width and height, serif and sans, and everything in-between so that people in remote parts of the world can create bad type in more than one dimension: like Century Expanded Condensed Sans Bold Outline Drop Shadow Oblique Small Caps Swash Superscript in Trumatch 32. You can even have a serif bullet…with a swash.

Electronic publishing is supposed to be anything that is non print and no one has yet put a value on the publishing part of the data highway. Billboards, toll booths, pot holes, road kill—eventually they will run out of metaphors and we can get down to business. Navigating the Internet is like driving at night with no lights, blindfolded with someone giving you directions in Bosnian. You can do anything on that data highway including religion? On Compuserve type GO: GOD or send a fax to the Israeli Phone Company and they will put it in the Wailing Wall direct to the Almighty.

Speaking of the Almighty, a recent article said that Microsoft sold only 6 million copies of Windows and this was not up to expectations. 6 million is not up to expectations!

CD-ROM publishing is a paradox. The CD-ROM standard has gone through three speed changes, plus CD-I and others. It's not that we do not have standards; we have too many standards. The pioneers who bought in early need to upgrade. They also bought into Beta video tape systems and 8-track cartridges, now gathering dust in the garage. My computer has magnetic hard disk storage, internal and external, floppy disk, both 2-1/2 and 5-1/4, 44 and 88mb Syquest, magneto optical, Bernoulli, CD-ROM, gigabyte hard drives and tape. I have unlisted SCSI addresses.

There's nothing wrong with being a pioneer. The definition of pioneer no longer deals with arrows: a pioneer is someone with a big garage.

CD-ROM publishers are unique. They count the copies they give away in their sales. Does General Motors know about this? They could triple their sales overnight

Much of what I see is multi-mediocrity. But the potential is enormous. When it is good, it is mindboggling. When it is bad, it is the norm. By the way, am I the only one willing to admit that I don't always understand Wired magazine? I have two sons. I lived through rock and roll and MTV. Too hip may also be unhip.

I was looking at a book from the 15th century the other day. No computer. No CD-ROM reader. Just a pair of old eyes. All these new publishing approaches seem to restrict rather than expand access to information. We are creating an information elite, sort of an artificial intelligensia. Paper and television are the media to reach mass markets. The company that finds a way to combine them will inherit the earth. If you want it. Ask for Jupiter.

My market used to be publishing and ink on paper products. Today we have printers who maintain databases, printers who stamp CD-ROMs, printers who produce multimedia. And by the way, they also put ink on paper or board or plastic or foil. Last year R.R. Donnelley paid more for disks of all kinds than they did for paper of all kinds. What then is a printer? What then is the printing industry?

We lost our user friendliness, if we ever had it. Windows users love to tell me how great their system is. I just ask them to key a pi symbol. And Microsoft and Apple: I will not write scripts. You will not make me a propeller head, techie, hacker, machead, computer jockey, geek or nerd. I have had to pump my own gas, bag my own groceries, and cut my own Christmas tree. I will not write code. You made computers friendly. Make coding friendly.

Gary Loveman, a professor at Harvard tried to measure the productivity gains that came with the billions of dollars invested in information technology. There was no positive effect he concluded. Where did our productivity go?

A lot of it was wasted watching that clock or hourglass on your screen. You stare at it because it will only take a second to switch back to the cursor. Ha! Or recovering from a bomb—"An error has occurred and everything you have ever known has been erased." Or loading the latest revision—"Turn off all inits, virus checkers, electrical appliances and any unclean thoughts." Or trying to connect a peripheral—"First, get a Phillips screwdriver and a degree from MIT…" It's all supposed to be so easy, until it doesn't work. I had a monitor to be repaired recently. It weighs a ton for something with a vacuum in it. They told me to ship it a thousand miles away.

It's like the annual model changes for automobiles until the Japanese taught us that a car could last until the last payment. Look at the names of new computers: Perfoma, Spectria, Presario. I expect Corinthian leather on the keys. Windows 95, Windows 96 Limited Edition. The revision of the month club.

Think back: We never read a magazine called Royal Typewriter User or attended an event called Carbon paper-

Ex or bought a book that told us the tips and tricks of White-Out (use a roller).

Or even subscribed to Number 2B Pencil World.

Marcia Peoples Halio at the University of Delaware described the Mac/PC gap in an article in *Academic Computing*. She noticed that Mac users became so enamored with the type and graphics that they tended to write at a lower academic level, while the PC users concentrated on the content rather than the form. That went out when Windows came in. Now everyone can write below their level.

Other academics argued that the we were going beyond mere language and for a much richer context, integrating other media into a new form of communication. Whenever something is said to be richer you have to be it to get it.

It always reminded me of Mark Twain and the typewriter. He supposedly typed a manuscript for his publisher who wrote back that he left out the punctuation. Twain sent a sheet filled with periods and commas and semicolons, etc. Insert where necessary, he said.

He eschewed the typewriter and went back to pencils and pads. He would love the program that digitizes your personal calligraphy so you can *type your handwriting*. Or the Personal Digital Assistant that translates handwriting to type so you can *write your typing*. Or voice recognition which eliminates both *writing and typing*. Or television, which eliminates writing, typing and even thinking. All you need is a thumb. ThumbWorld.

In the 1872 James Clephane said "I want to bridge the gap between the typewriter and the printed page." Now every desktop computer has the ability to bridge that gap—over a cable to the laser printer or imagesetter or digital color press. (A new ink jet printer has permanent ink but the machine fades away.) Word processing, document processing, and even image processing moved away from proprietary systems and onto the desktop. Remember Vydec and

Redactron and Lexitron and Linolex and CPT and even Wang? Gone with the winds of change.

Apple, IBM, and Microsoft—the new Axis. They may be similar to the global superpowers in Orwell's *1984,* shifting alliances faster than Winston Smith could change recorded history. Today we have a trade press to do that. The only truth is the truth of the moment—we do not learn from the past because we are preoccupied by the future. *Apple is forming an alumni association for past presidents, but the Super Dome is booked for the next few years.*

Why get angry with Microsoft because it's so big—IBM was big once. What's new? What's next? We can expect:

New programs.	New stuff.
Revised programs.	More stuff.
Other programs.	Upgrades.
Other releases.	Revisions.
New models.	More.
Newer models.	Still more.
Other operating systems.	Better.
Newer operating systems.	Big.
New computers	Bigger.
Other computers.	Cheap.
Better printers.	Cheaper.
Bigger printers.	New.
Cheaper printers.	Newer.
Bigger, better *and* cheaper printers.	Now.

So what market are we in? Darned if I know. It no longer has a name.

We do have a level playing field now. It is no longer IBM versus Apple. It is Microsoft versus everyone else. Corporate America did not accept the Macintosh because there was only one supplier. Maybe they know of other suppliers of Windows. To run all the new software will require faster, beefier computers. It will make no difference which supplier you buy from. All that will matter is productivity and user efficiency and ROI. MIS managers of the world: wake up and smell the Apples.

Random Bits About the Contradictions of Computer Life

My kid is the only one who can set up the censorship chip for blocking TV shows from kids. He also opens child-proof bottle caps.

Do you put your password on a Post-It note stuck to your monitor.

To buy most products, there is an 800 number. For support, the phone number is unlisted.

Multitasking: the ability of more than one program to crash at the same time.

Personalization: the ability to customize communication to people you do not know, about things they do not care about, in colors they cannot distinguish.

If at first you don't succeed, call it version 2.0.

I have a Control key but I'm not in control.

My answering machine never has any answers.

There is a fine line between mousing and looking like an idiot.

Can a general-purpose computer do anything specific?

God: Life has just ended. Press any key...

The abacus hasn't changed in 1,000 years. Darn those upgrades

Surveys indicate that most people do not like surveys.

What if there were no hypothetical questions?

Cybernauts travel in cyberspace and wind up in cyberia.

Networks let other people crash your computer.

The Abbot of Sponheim

About 40 years after the invention of moveable type, the Abbot of Sponheim, Germany published an impassioned book called "In Praise of Scribes," extolling the glory of handwritten books. As head of a large scriptorium he argued that scribes should continue to copy manuscripts despite the advent of printing because of the need for diligence and devotion exercised in the process. He also said that hand-copied words on parchment would last centuries beyond the printed words on paper.

To get his message out, the good Abbot had the book printed. The scribes took too long, we guess. He used a new technology to promote an old technology. The Abbot of Sponheim is a metaphor for contradiction.

He would appreciate:

- The postmasters of America using e-mail.
- The Postal Service Web site.
- The parts catalog for a Heidelberg press on CD-ROM.
- Disks for America Online & Compuserve in magazines.
- Print ads for World Wide Web sites.
- TV commercials for magazines.
- Radio spots for Miracle Ear.
- Books on how to read.
- Wired magazine in print.
- Any TV commercial that ends with "Call for a free brochure…"

Today, we live in a world of contradiction, in a nation that produces smart bombs and dumb kids—hesitant to embrace new technology at the expense of old technology.

Just once I would like a machine to be in use at the end of its depreciation period. IRS was not happy when I claimed 10 days for a PC.

Standard: the unknowing determining the unuseable for the unbelieving.

The Net is Not a Life

Some see the Internet as the embodiment of the future of communication, and if it provides universal access, it will. But more people are writing about the net than actually using it.

Back at the time of the Abbot of Sponheim, only a privileged few could afford any kind of book. Today Internet access rests with those earning $67,000 year or more. Just as the book and other forms of print became more democratic, so must Internet access. Gutenberg's invention made lead more valuable than gold because virtually everyone understood what print could do. No one really knows what the so-called information superhighway can do.

For print to be displaced as the primary means of communication, you must replace it with as pervasive a communication channel. Cable TV does not do it. Broadcast TV is close. The Internet is not even close. It is more or less electronic graffiti on the info highway.

"Surf the web" says a lot about people with attention deficit disorder. The Internet could be a network of networks with a few million people with short attention spans and too much idle time searching for the ultimate diversion. Most Internet users are white males under 24 and popular sites involve erotica. The reason: no staples.

The Internet is like CB radio, only you have to type. It's nothing to e-mail home about. How do you make money on the Internet: This guy ran magazine ads for years telling you how he got rich and for $20 he would tell you the secret. I sent the 20 bucks and got a booklet telling me to run magazine ads on how I got rich by charging $20 for the same information. More people will make more money telling other people how to make money than real users will, trying to make money by actually doing something. Another oxymoron: net profits. Some say cyberspace is a parallel universe. Get a parallel life.

Windows dressing

Sure there are more PCs than Macs. The meek will inherit the earth, right? Or is it: the geek will inherit the earth? The copy said "Requires Windows 3.1 or better" so I bought a Macintosh. Whoever said Windows 95 really is Macintosh

89 is right. The Windows95 hype was so overwhelming that I bought a copy even though I don't own a PC. Bill Gates was right—my productivity went up immediately. I'm afraid to open the box and become too efficient. Instead of a trash barrel, Windows95 has a recycling bin. A pc PC in the age of political correctness. You put text into one, pictures in another.

Let us not ignore Apple. Their new Powerbook bursts into flames. They have now concluded that this is a feature. Microsoft says it will not be out-burst and says Windows96 will not only burst into flames but will also play the "Stars and Stripes Forever."

Microsoft paid a million dollars or more for the rights to "Start me up" by the Rolling Stones. Maybe they should have gotten "I don't get no satisfaction."

Not a verb—a nerb

"Re-purpose" This industry has done more to make nouns into adjectives and verbs than any other. A "nerb" is a noun used as a verb:

To apple: to incorrectly predict production of a popular product. (I often hear "Apple only has 10% of the market." I think that Apple has made a decision to *only* have 10% of the market by limiting production).

To xerox: to innovate relentlessly and market occasionally. Where's the color Docutech, folks?

To at&t: to divide and conquer The three new AT&T companies will further divide into three companies. Then they will be eligible for the MCI friends and families rate.

The difference between Mac users and PC users?

1. PC users drive Chevys. Mac users drive Toyotas.

2. PC users watch Fox. Mac users watch PBS.

3. PC users live in apartments. Mac users live in condos.

4. PC users eat burgers Mac users eat quiche

5. PC users go to Disneyland.
Mac users *create* Disneyland.

Media Madness

There is print. To get to print faster, we have computer-to-film and now computer-to-dry film. But computer-to-film is under attack by computer-to-plate and computer-to-dry plate. But computer-to-plate is under attack by computer-to-press and computer-to-digital printer.

Then there is non print. To eliminate print we record documents on CD-ROM in portable document formats, but CD-ROM needs more capacity so it is under attack by new high volume read-only disks and DVD disks. And CD-ROM is itself under attack by totally electronic delivery, like the Internet.

We want to reduce paper use but more people are buying more paper for their desktop printers. Instead of one printing press making a million of something, a million presses are making one. That's short run.

Print isn't dead.

It just seems that way because it doesn't do anything.

The irony of technology

- If you find a replacement part, you will not find the tool.
- If you remove the bad part, you will not find a replacement.
- If the dealer does have a replacement, it's not needed.
- If the dealer has a replacement and it is needed, it will be the wrong one.
- The cost of a replacement part exceeds a new system.
- If the disk is big enough, there's not enough memory.
- If there's enough memory, the disk is inadequate.
- If both are adequate, the operating system won't support them.
- If all are OK, the system speed is inadequate.
- If you need an expansion card, there is no slot.
- If there is a slot, there is no card.
- No matter what device you buy, it will not have the right cable.
- If the disk is repaired, only the list of files remains to remind you what was lost.
- Broken systems will always work in the presence of a repair person.

Couch Potatoes versus Virtual Vegetables

We have a generation of couch potatoes who mindlessly surf through 88 channels of television. We are also raising a generation who sit mindlessly in front of their computer and surf the web. I give you Virtual Vegetables, people who spend more time in cyberspace than they do in reality.

Virtual reality: It used to be called imagination.

- The couch potato has a TV remote control.
The virtual vegetable has a mouse

- The couch potato surfs cable channels.
The virtual vegetable surfs the net.

- The couch potato gets up for food.
The virtual vegetable gets up for nature

- The couch potato watches 9 hours of TV a week.
The virtual vegetable computes for 13 hours a week

- The couch potato gets repetitive stress injury.
The virtual vegetable—hemorrhoids.

Around and around

The demo was impressive.	So I bought the program
The program was un-intuitive.	So I read the manual
The manual was ponderous.	So I tried the Help file
The Help file was not helpful.	So I bought the book
The book re-wrote the manual.	So I went to the exhibition
The exhibition was too crowded.	So I watched the video
The video was thumbs down.	So I took the course
The course was too shallow.	So I tried the seminar
The seminar was too short.	So I subscribed to the newsletter
The newsletter had no news.	Until they announced a revision.

The demo was impressive . . .

10 Signs You're Spending Too Much Time With a Computer

10: Your computer is your significant other.
9: You dream in Netscape and hyperlink to other people's dreams. Except for users of Navigator who link best to Microsoft dreams.
8: Your hand has the permanent shape of a mouse.
7: You went from"Show ID" to "Senior's discount" and recall very little in-between.
6: You surf the web naked.
5: You try to attach e-mail to the refrigerator.
4: Your home page is "worst of the web"—your home is worst of the neighborhood.
3: You give new meaning to the term SCSI.
2: You read the alt.sex newsgroup and vaguely remember what it's about.
1: You tell disagreeable people to "Kiss my gif".

An irrecoverable error has occurred and you have been erased.

It is the Year 2096
The Dawn of a New Error

Microsoft reintroduces Windows 95 and reuses the packaging saved from the previous iteration which only sold a billion copies, which was not up to expectations.

Microsoft has acquired IBM, AT&T and the U.S. Department of Justice.

President of the United States William Gates instructs *his* Justice Department to investigate IBM for predatory marketing of OS2/95.

The Postal Service is a division of R.R. Donnelley, which now represents 80% of the printing industry. Everyone has their own personal Zip code.

High-fidelity printing is so realistic, it is reality. Using special organic inks and edible paper, microwavable meals are printed.

Xerox has merged with a company that has placed a combination Docutech and Port-A-Potty on every street corner. There is still a use for paper.

Some of us have little signs on our forehead that say "Intel inside"

Consumers start a new trend by demanding printed versions of their audio and video disks. Retail operations arise to sell manually processed media. They are called bookstores.

Digital images are now holograms, projecting computer images of reality on demand. Lonely people go steady with inflatable holograms.

Instead of gold or silver, the world economy is based on paper. Reams are stored in Fort Knox. Counterfeiters make illegal sized paper.

Newspapers once printed a code in the TV listings to automate the taping of certain shows at certain times. Now, TV flash codes to tell you which newspaper articles and books to read and copy.

Personalized color printing has reached new heights. Everyone has their own personal postage stamp. It eliminates the need for return addresses.

It is discovered that DNA is the source code to a Microsoft program. Pay up or you will be revised.

Wired magazine still makes money the old fashioned way—printed magazines.

The Food & Drug Administration bans the Internet as an addictive drug.

Every one on earth has their own home page. Mine is sponsored by Twinkies.

Adobe Systems finally runs out of companies to acquire.

Senator Packwood still harasses women but does not remember why.

A killer web site is discovered. Net surfers die of boredom waiting for a 5 gigabyte picture to load.

Congress passes a law abolishing illness and eliminates Medicare as unnecessary.

Every computer and every program finally reach perfection and no longer bomb. A comet hits the earth and wipes out humanity. The dinosaurs return.

I leave you with an actual quote from Leonid Krapchuk, president of the Ukraine, and it may describe our industry, whatever it is:

> "Today we stand at the edge of a great abyss."
> "Tomorrow, we take a giant step forward."

The Future

Just draw a trend line from every new technology showing it going up and every old technology going down. More memory, more disks, bigger scanners, more gray levels, more dpi, more fonts, more color, more MIPS and megahertz, faster communications, more bandwidth, computer to anything and everything, delivered on demand, immediate, even yesterday. Now, try to teach changing technology to a workforce on the move. Let's look into the real future:

Professor Frank Romano IV looked at his wall and started talking. He leaned back in his personal ergonomic chair/workstation as it adjusted itself to his shift in body weight (with accompanying changes in heat and massage) and called up an open text window for dictation for his latest book. The entire wall of his home office was a flat-screen high-resolution liquid crystal display. The almost holographic image that he had been watching was a beach in the Virgin Islands with the muted sounds of surf and sea birds in the distance. Outside it was snowing on the eve of the Third Millennium and people were predicting dire consequences of the Y3K bug.

Voice recognition was now a commonplace approach and most people could not type. The major impediment had been solved with the adoption of the standardized Victor Borge punctuation system back at the turn of the Second Millennium. As he spoke the system automatically converted voice to text, performing an extensive contextual analysis to differentiate between "red" and "read" for example. Small sound effects were used for special symbols and functions. He called for a bullet by placing his index finger in his cheek and snapping it out very fast.

Spelling, grammar, legal, and politically correct analyses were run. Instead of he or she, the neutral xe was used for all pronouns. Feedback was almost instantaneous and comments from colleagues were received in additional text windows accompanied by voice annotation. All changes were incorporated in the copy and the text was completed. It would automatically pick up the format, including kerning, tracking and hyphenation preferences. The art department received the text and began its layout and design.

Collections of sample pages and award winners had become electronic in the last century. A search was made through the last five years to find pages with related themes and an electronic bibliography was completed. These were reviewed and the process of page assembly began.

Image banks of digital images were consulted and several individual images were selected. Automatic billing and royalty arrangements were made. The images and text were merged with design elements to complete the pages. They were then returned to the professor who commented and approved the final versions. The data was released to a production data bank for dissemination alternatives. Publications were routinely prepared for multiple media: print, disk and UWW (the Universal Wide Web had been expanded with the colonization of Mars).

Subscribers could receive their publication as several alternative forms of media. The most popular was the DUD for Digital Ultimate Disk, about the size of an Oreo cookie which could contain several terabytes of information. Subscribers could also call up the publication on their own wall displays and lastly, there was print. It had been discovered that pulp was a nutritious form of protein and fibre and that it was better to eat it than read it. Those items still printed used a form of paper made from seaweed and reprocessed trash, printed with ink made from cranberry juice and crabgrass. Print was truly organic.

Publications in print had been mailed by the Postal Service, now owned by Quebecor-World-Donnelley, using a new 23-digit Zip code, plus four. A new DNA coded system was being developed that addressed every human being on earth directly. Publications were bound using a new electronic paper melding technique. Since 2050 the use of blown-in reply cards was made a Federal crime.

Actually, most printing was done at corner kiosks which had replaced bookstores, where subscribers went and requested their publications from touch screens or voice panels. Each unit was personalized to the subscriber using demographic, credit card, checkout counter bar code, and buying pattern data. For those who still wanted a book, it was printed while they waited at combination coffee shops and bookstores (instead of bookstores with coffee shops).

Advertising was still present. A consolidation movement had affected every industry (there was only one automobile company: General Toyota) and IBM (the M stood for Microsoft) was now a commonwealth that claimed title to Greenland. Ads were developed and disseminated electronically by the major galactic agency, J. Olgilvy Saatchi.

Since all material was in electronic form, printers took the data files and bypassed both film and plates, going directly to new electronic presses that used electronic tink (a blend of toner and ink). The entire system was automatic through binding and mailing. Mail was routed via the nationwide underground pneumatic distribution system which eliminated all trucks from highways, where automobiles were now controlled by computers, not drivers. California was threatening to secede from the Union over this system.

Publications were now routinely produced with staffs of one or two. All communication was electronic. Voice and image messages could be left and many decisions could be made without the participants actually talking to one another. Those little "while you were out" slips were discontinued since everyone was out but always in contact. Workers left their personal workstations but carried subminiature, genetically inserted cell-phone-pager-computer units which provided audio, visual, and other forms of sensory feedback. The Palm Pilot had become the Fingertip Pilot. All workstation chairs had an infinite number of adjustments for heat, recline, massage, sound, music, and other levels of comfort.

Portable systems integrated miniature antennas which communicated worldwide using orbital satellites. Tiny chips were inserted at the genetic level at birth giving every human being their own ID number. As you passed by giant liquid crystal signs and billboards, the messages were specifically oriented to you. Frank recalled passing one recently that reminded him of his wife's birthday.

The concept of work was now primarily cerebral since robots did most of the manufacturing and service tasks. There was no money as such and all financial transactions were via retinal eye scan. Counterfeit contact lenses were still a problem. At restaurants a small ceremony was held at the end of each meal as carbon paper was torn onto a silver tray. No one could recall why.

News was instantaneous and personalized to the desires of the individual. Congress still had not balanced the budget and Mideast peace talks had stalled again on the color of the tablecloth.

The work day was only three hours. The work week was only four days. In their spare time people travelled widely without leaving home. The use of virtual reality meant that they could interface with a holographic video and become a part of it. The sensations of walking down (or swimming down) a street in Venice were as real as actually being there.

Education was all by distance learning. Students could connect from anywhere and join virtual classes. Texts were electronic and students could have print, screen data, or have the book read to them while they slept, which was most of the time. The professor was presented as a holographic image and could use an electronic blackboard, presentation program, or many multimedia alternatives. Students still had assignments, which had to be delivered in electronic forms. New excuses were developed to keep pace with technology, as in "The dog erased my disk drive."

Students could study under any professor at any university in the world. Most college campuses had been converted into entertainment centers (owned by Sony-Universal-Dreamworks).

The teaching of changing technology was still a challenge, but now all schools were equal in that all had access to the same technology, which was online. With the advent of virtual reality, any situation or system could be simulated electronically. Once a year students and teachers were encouraged to actually meet face to face since travel was now phasing over to new "Star Trek" transporter technology, owned by American-Continental-United, which no longer lost luggage, but could lose body organs.

The professor leaned back in his workstation and changed the display image to a snow-covered trail in Colorado. He dreamed of other times when students and teachers met within four brick walls not in cyberspace. The evolution of communication and publishing was becoming the farthest thing from his mind. He switched on the virtual reality mode and went skiing.

The Computer Made Me Do It

Computer programs are said to be electronic manifestations of biologic entities that inhabit computer memory. Scientists want to use what they are calling artificial life to answer the question: how does nature create order out of chaos. First, nature hires a management consultant. Then, nature forms a committee. Finally, there is chaos.

Archeologists have just discovered caves in southern France with well-preserved prehistoric wall drawings. These are somewhat special in that they represent early Cro-Magnon impressionism. It's not a hairy mammoth, it's an impression of a hairy mammoth.

Just think: with fax publishing we finally get the subscriber to pay for the paper and the press. Of course, fax modems let you receive paperless faxes. Paper companies can then introduce faxless paper, or paperless paper, or even stealth paper.

The real personal digital assistant: The Power PC...the Power Mac...and now...the Power Pencil. It produces text and graphics, writes in any language, is extremely user friendly, and has a high level of portability. Operating system? Me!

The real mobile phone: Forget about cellular phones and let's go right to chromosomal telephony. You just think of the person you want to call and you are connected with that person instantly, no matter where they are on the planet. There is no such thing as a wrong number; it is now a wrong person. A busy signal means they took themselves off the hook, or they are dead. Be careful, hackers will be able to break into your mind. What's next: chromosomal answering machines.

The result will be instantaneous universal consciousness, or zen communication. Then each of us will need a zen code.

Tried a voice recognition system recently and inadvertently sneezed into the microphone. The computer produced a screenful of s's and said gezuntheit.

Artificial life; artificial intelligence....and now...artificial government. Bundled with Microsoft Office is Microsoft Government. There are 535 possible style sheets, each with an infinite number of variations, but these can be overridden by one main dialog box, unless it has the line item edit, or modified by nine menus with black borders. Input can be by keyboard, political action committee, or lobbyist.

They call it invisible technology. Computers are so small that the only thing visible is the screen. Eventually the screens will be invisible and images will be projected. That will give us screenless screens. Voice recognition will give us keyless keyboards, and then finally the industry will move to computerless computers. And you will not have to be present to operate the system, which leads to peopleless offices.

What is the difference between an expert, an authority, and a consultant? The expert knows a lot about something. The authority knows a lot about everything. The consultant knows a lot about everything else. If you are more than one of these you are really in trouble.

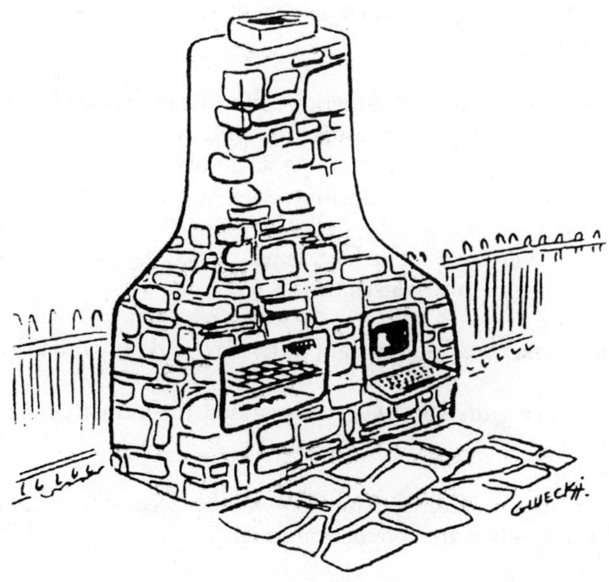

Knowledge Workers of the World: Unite!

The newest of the new buzz terms is "information manufacturing" which probably takes place in an information factory, with knowledge workers toiling on assembly lines for information products:

The icon for this new world is a light bulb with a little person over it, lit up.

The information assembly line had to shut down because of a shortage of data.

Information workers take mental breaks.

The fitness center lets you leap to an opinion.

A memory lapse is an occupational hazard for a knowledge worker.

A penny for your thoughts is the minimum sage.

When knowledge workers go on strike, their picket signs have footnotes.

The major threat to the American information worker will be off-shore intelligence manufacturing. Low quality information is being manufactured by slave laborers in Asia and sweat shop workers in the Bronx.

OSHA will investigate accidents caused by knowledge workers who raise consciousness without a truss.

One worker was put on light duty. He could only muse.

A worker with ESP was reprimanded for industrial espionage.

The statue of Rodin's "Thinker" was replaced with a statue of a committee, in a pondering pose.

Mind workers' motto: Think or thwim.

You can have any kind of information you want so long as it is black.

The company motto now really means something: "Think."

Toffler says that most workers will be mind workers doing mind work. A mind is a terrible thing to lay off.

A union will be formed: the United Mind Workers of America. When they strike, they will stop thinking.

Will there be mind breaks and mind vacations? Will we lose mind jobs to other countries that have subsidized mind work?

Will Detroit be the mind work center of the United States? Will the Big Three automakers convert over to mind work and then complain because we import more mind products from Japan?

Q: Where do mind workers work?
A: Intellectual property.

When information workers decide to stop work they also stop thinking and take a cognitation break.

At breaks they exercise together by jumping to conclusions.

An entry level position would be manual rather than mental: "paper pusher."

Workers toil for 7.5 hours to output a memo, albeit a long memo.

Losing concentration could become an occupational hazard.

The union says a penny for your thoughts is actually below minimum wage.

Quality control. You can hear the inspectors accepting or rejecting work: "Good idea." Bad idea." "Good idea."

When knowledge workers go on strike, their picket signs are blank, set in stealth Souvenir.

The information assembly line had to shut down because of a shortage of assumptions.

One worker was fired for having unproductive thoughts.

The major threat to the American information worker will be off-shore intelligence manufacturing. However, there is no tariff on any stupidity being imported.

OSHA will investigate accidents caused by workers who have lofty thoughts without a forklift.

A worker with Extra Sensory Perception was reprimanded for industrial espionage.

The other symbol for this new world is a light bulb with a little computer over it, with a light bulb on the screen.

FedEx delivers an idea whose time has come.

Supervisors are told that a digital display is not a hand gesture.

New motto: I e-mail; therefore, I am.

Who Does the Work?

U.S. population	200,000,000
Retired	– 84,000,000
That leaves 116,000,000 to do the work	
In school	– 75,000,000
That leaves 41,000,000 to do the work	
Federal government employees	– 22,000,000
That leaves 19,000,000 to do the work	
Armed forces	– 4,000,000
That leaves 15,000,000 to do the work	
State, city, municipal employees	– 14,700,000
That leaves 300,000 to do the work	
In hospitals	– 180,000
That leaves 120,000 to do the work	
In prison	– 119,999
That leaves 30 to do the work	

29 of you are sitting around.

And here I am to do the work.

By the Numbers

It is truly a brave new world. When our publication turned 20 years old, I received e-mail from 80 or so people who responded to an article I wrote. My first reaction was: who ever dreamed we would communicate this way back in 1977? How our world has changed. Ponder this:

1. 40% of U.S. households now control 70% of the disposable income. These tend to be more affluent, educated Americans with access to the latest technology and the latest information.

2. Of total personal consumption, 6.7% goes for movies, theater and sports, 2.2% goes for magazines, .8% for newspapers, and 1.9% for books. 62% of all adults read a newspaper daily and 75% of all adults read a newspaper at least once a week. U.S. adults read or scan an average of 10 magazines a month. We *watch* more than we *read*.

3. Most of us have only about 3,500 hours per year of personal time that can be devoted to reading, TV, listening to music, etc. That includes weekends, holidays and vacation, plus whatever you can grab during the work week. Thus, new media compete with old media for our attention.

4. Cost per thousand baud telecommunications was $500 in 1980 and was about $20 in 1997. Eventually it may be cheaper to transmit information than to record or print and deliver it to you. CD- and DVD-ROM could yield to online delivery over time. Bandwidth is everything.

5. In 1986 every encyclopedia published was only in print. Today, 5% are in print, 45% on CD-ROM, 40% on a CD-ROM bundled with your new personal computer, and 10% accessed over the WWW. The encyclopedia is essentially free for some people. Eventually 100% of all encyclopedias could be digital.

6. People who work at or from home for any amount of time represented 28% of the workforce in 1988; in 1997 41%. It will hit 50% by 2000. Not all are home offices as such.

7. Students per computer in 1984 averaged 125; today it is under 9. More people are entering the workforce with computer skills. Eventually, they will not be able to enter the workforce *without* computer skills.

8. The average number of working hours per week in 1964 was 38; today it is 52. There are more 2-person wage

earners in a family and the home office is an extension of the real office. We work harder. We need to work smarter.

9. U.S. movie ticket revenues were $6 billion in 1995. One out of four U.S. adults goes to the movies once a month. But they rent one video cassette a week as well. U.S. bookstore sales: $12 billion, 24% of which is sold in two summer months. I guess you still can't read the computer out of doors.

10. Average daily household television *on* time is 6 hours and 39 minutes. This number is actually rising and represents 2,427 hours out of the 3,500 hours of personal time available. We actually watch the TV an average of five hours a day. On weekdays, adults listen to the radio for an average of 3 hours and 20 minutes, in many cases, in their automobiles.

11. One in ten households has a desktop computer with a modem. In 1995 the number of e-mail messages exceeded the number of print mail messages transmitted in the U.S.

12. In only 7% of U.S. households is the TV only for broadcast reception. In most, the TV is connected to cable, video cassette recorder/player and/or a video game system. It is not too difficult to predict that the TV will become a window to the Internet.

13. 72% of American teens have a CD player. Each of us spends $55 a year on recorded music. Actually my kids more than cover their share.

14. 31% of American teens have a home computer. Just because it is in the home does not mean it is available for business use. Both kids and parents will compete for the computer...and the TV.

15. Average life expectancy for men today is 63; in 2010: 67. For women, 67 and 71. If we develop a customer they may be around for a long time.

16. Worldwide population of personal computers is now 250 million; by 2010 over 400 million. Most are too old to do what we want to do today.

17. Number of McDonald's fast food restaurants: 14,000; by 2010: 30,000. We want what we want when we want it. The same will be true of information.

18. Gambling revenues in 1994 were $39.5 billion. By 2010 it is expected to be $126.6 billion. Wanna bet?

19. There are 1,200 communications satellites in orbit. In 2000 there will be over 2,000. Everyone will be able to connect ...at the same time.

20. Of all the people ever born on the planet Earth, 51% are now alive. That's why you can't find a parking space when you really need it.

The Law of Systems

(First Law of Systems)
Systems do not work.

This is apparent from empirical evidence—observation of the real world (is there an unreal world?). Remember when some ditch digger cut a cable in New Jersey and air traffic control got disrupted and planes were landing on the Jersey Turnpike.

(Appearances Are Deceiving Rule)
If systems do work,
it is because they only seem to work.

Not working is the norm. When something actually works it is an abnormality and should be checked out immediately. Call support.

(The Amoeba Principle)
Parts of a system are as bad as the entire system.

Just because the people in your local post office appear efficient, do not project this to the entire system. Just because that long distance call went through does not mean that it will happen again.

(Second Theory of Inclusiveness)
Everything is part of a system.

You cannot escape systems. They are pervasive. There is no a part of our society—including our society—that is not systems related.

(First Footnote to Second Theory)
Therefore, everything does not work.

It's that simple. This extends from the unseen world to the known world. Machines are systems. Animals are systems. There is nothing that is not a system, although Amtrak is pretty close.

(Law of Galactic Consciousness)
The universe is a system.

As in "solar system." The atom has little things revolving around a central thing. The universe has planets revolving around a sun. Same principle, just bigger.

(Galactic Unconsciousness)
The universe does not work.

Maybe it worked once, when it started but that was a long time ago and then there was a big bang. Which no one was around to hear. So maybe there wasn't a big bang.

(Cyber Creationism)
New systems create new problems.

New systems create new problems. Old systems create new problems. Teenage systems want to borrow the car.

(Let Sleeping Systems Lie Law)
When setting up a new system, be careful not to disturb a system that might inadvertently be working.

America Online went to implement a new computer program and took the entire system down for 15 hours. AT&T had the same problem and the east coast lost long distance service.

(Einstein's Last Words)
Systems absorb time^2.

No matter how much time you had when you started, the critical part of the project will come down to the last ten minutes.

(Einstein's Proof)
There is never enough time.

Einstein died before he could prove it. His investigation found that there is only a certain amount of time in the entire universe and it is being used up at a rapid rate.

(Newton's Last Law)
Systems evolve, but not enough to matter.

Systems always change—like living organisms. But living organisms usually die; however, some kinds of systems live forever. Bureaucracy is eternal.

(Hawking's Hypothesis)
The universe, space, and time are related, but distantly.

That about covers everything. Of course, Einstein said it first and now he's dead.

(The Republican Manifesto)
The universe will someday be rationed.

There will not be enough universe to go around. There will not be enough time to go around. Galactic coupons will be distributed.

(The Petunia Principle)
Systems grow.

Systems tend to grow in complexity rather than in simplification, until the resulting unreliability becomes intolerable. Unfortunately, you cannot see them growing until it is too late.

(Third Postulate of Cosmic Expansionism)
Systems grow to encompass the known universe.

Nothing is local. Everything is interconnected. A fly beats its wings in Borneo and a hurricane threatens the Yucatan Peninsular.

(Chaos Algorithm)
The more vital the system, the greater the probability of catastrophic systems failure.

The most critical system will fail given that the fail-safe part of the system will eventually fail.

(The 80-20 Rule)
The smaller the system, the greater the probability of systems failure, but there will be less harm.

Maybe.

(The Grecian Formula)
The bigger the system, the narrower the role of human beings.

Like turning the system on and off.

(The Oligarchy Axiom)
Systems are like mobs of people; they cannot be managed.

Like herding cats.

(Peter's Paradox)
Complex systems produce complex results.

Simply put, that's about right.

(Peter's Conundrum)
Simple systems produce complex results.

Simply put, that's about right, too.

(The Empirical Definitive)
Complex results cannot be evaluated by human beings.

Because they are too simple.

(The Quantum Quandary)
Systems do not produce useful solutions.

Any system will have at least two applications; any system will have at least two exceptions. They cannot be the same.

If you want to predict

(Gumpian Logic)
A system is like a box of chocolates.
You never know what you're going to get.

Surprise, surprise, the system just bombed.

(Simple Simon Logic)
Simple systems might produce simple results,
but these are, in and of themselves, simply unuseable.

A qumquat is a simple system. Most fruit are simple systems. Vegetables are complex.

(The Paramecium Principle)
Simple systems that grow to become complex systems
have no simple system characteristics and thus
produce no simple results.

Because simple is as simple does.

(The Law of Simplicity)
All systems are complex.

Because simple systems are complex systems is disguise: the phantom of the operating system.

(The Law of Predictability)
System results are unpredictable.

Once you open a can of worms, the only way to re-can them is to use a larger can.

(Artificial Intelligence)
Human actions in systems are unpredictable.

Where the system is concerned, do not ask Why? Humans are placed within systems to add a measure of unpredictability. We think that we are in control, when actually we do what the system wants us to do.

the future...invent it.

(Real Intelligence)
Machine actions in systems are unpredictable.

Machines are also unpredictable but in more predictable ways. Or, predictable in unpredictable ways.

(The Punctuation Fallacy)
Human and machine actions are unpredictable, period.

Any system which depends on the reliability of people is unreliable. Any system that depends on the reliability of machines is unreliable.

(The Prevarication Principle)
Systems do not do what they say they are doing.

Systems do not have an ethical base.

(The Second Dichotomy of Relativism)
A function performed by a big system is not identical to a function with the same name performed by a small system.

That's why they are called aliases.

(Virtual Unreality)
Reality is what the system says it is.

What you see on the screen is your world.

(Unstated Law of Attraction)
Systems attract people who like systems.

Less like a fan club and more like a cult.

(Geek Chic)
People who like systems are like systems.

Fingers positioned on keyboards represents an act of subservience.

(The Brute Force Force)
A system either works or not; it cannot be forced to work; although guaranteed overtime and health care benefits would be an incentive.

Systems do what they darn well want to do.

(The Accidental Theorist)
Some systems could in fact work by accident, but do not.

Most accidents in the best of systems involve two or more events of low probability occurring in the worst possible combination at the worst possible time.

(The Garbo Axiom)
If a system is broken and works, leave it alone.

Never test for a system error that you don't know how to handle.

(Kafka's Hypothesis)
New systems are as bad as old systems, and vice versa.

Systems are ageless.

(The Holmesian Principle)
Malfunctioning systems may never be detected.

Because malfunction is the norm.

(Darwinian Dogma)
Fail-safe systems also fail.

Fail-safe means they are safe to fail.

(Knowledge Theory)
Systems are beyond human comprehension.

Human comprehension is beyond human comprehension.

(Motion Theory)
Systems have their own inertia.

Once in motion, they stay in motion unless they come to a red light.

(Newton's Footnote)
A system in motion tends to stay in motion.

Until you pull the plug.

(Last Law of Inevitability)
A system at rest will not remain at rest and will still grow and will still be a failure, so there.

Like black holes, systems simultaneously suck in resources and shrink in terms of production. An increase in expenditure will be matched by a fall in production.

(The Browning Rhyme)
Complex systems can fail in an infinite number of ways.

Let me count them…

(The Cybersoul Syndrome)
Systems behave as if they had a will to live.

The system is a sacred tin god: never break it or dent it when you can get what you want by bending it. However, it will snap back.

(The Kevorkian Challenge)
Systems do not die and will not kill themselves.

They must be killed by human beings with a magnet in the shape of a cross.

Those who know *how*, work

(The Law of Oz)
Great advances do not result from systems designed to produce great advances.

The result of advanced systems is advanced results. The resulting advance

(MIT Graffiti)
Systems suck.

Engineers have a way with words, with footnotes, no less.

(Hierarchical Homily)
If a system does not provide a benefit for each individual in the information chain, the information will be corrupted at their level, and degrade through the chain.

I think that says things go from bad to worse.

(Cybertheory)
People perceive machines and systems as people. Machines perceive machines and people alike.

To a computer, a Cuisinart is God. Cuisinarts are agnostic.

(Take A Number)
One person's red tape is another person's system.

In a bureaucratic system, useless work displaces useful work.

(The Bozo Conundrum)
The more ridiculous a system, the higher the probability of its success.

Self-checking systems check their own reliability. Sure! And the inmates run the asylum.

for those who know *why*.

The ROM in the PROM

If a packet hits a pocket on a socket on a port,
And the web is interrupted 'cause the wire has a short,
When access to the network makes your RAID array abort,
Don't knock it when the socket pocket packet has an error to report.

If your Finder finds a file format followed by a flash,
And double clicking icons put your window in the trash,
Your data is corrupted 'cause the file folders clash,
The situation's hopeless and the system's gonna crash!

Check the label on the cable on the gable of your house,
If the Internet's connected to a button on your mouse
To enable an unstable state of data ins and outs,
Then the table isn't able and there aren't any doubts

When the copy of your floppy gets sloppy on the disk,
And the microcode instructions cause unnecessary RISC,
'Cause the instruction in the manual has a noted asterisk
And the service representative keeps muttering a "tsk"

If your packets want to tunnel to another protocol,
That's repeatedly rejected by the printer down the hall.
And the tech rep says you need a really clean install
Just hang it up forever and take a trip down to the mall

Remember When...?

A computer was something from a sci-fi movie of note
A window required Windex and ram was related to goat

Meg was short for Margaret and gigs were jobs at nights
Now they all mean different things and that really mega bytes

An application helped you get a job
A program was a TV show
A cursor used profanity
A keyboard was a piano

Memory was something that you lost with age
And what you saw on a screen was not a page
A CD was a bank account
And a 3" floppy was no one's business but yours

Compress was something you did to the garbage
Not something you did to a file
And unzip anything in public you'd be in jail for awhile
Logon was adding wood to the fire
Hard drive was a long trip on the road
A mouse pad was where a mouse lived
And a backup happened in your toilet

Cut you did with a pocket knife
Paste you did with glue
A web site was a spider's home
And a virus was the flu

I guess I'll stick to my pad and paper
And the memory in my head
I hear nobody's been killed in a computer crash
but when it happens they wish they were dead

Instructions Included

Instructions you need to straighten out your computer: Find the screen thing and make the pointing thing go over it and move the mouse thingy while you click on the whatsit, the left whatsit, not the right whatsit, then move the little movy thing on the screen down to the third thingamagiggy that looks like a picture of a picture. Highlight the little gizmo, not the big gizmo, and copy and paste to the clip-whatchamacallit. It will take you to another box thingy with another little picture gizmo. You can then see the name of what you want to install. Then you have to click twice with the mouse whatsit and this will open the program. If you click the wrong thing the computer will go blank. If you miss a step go back and trace your steps. And remember, if it doesn't work for you, you can go back to the setup, and un-install the gizmo by reversing the entire setup thru the highlight and paste method. This works for me every time!

The 10 Laws of IT

IT is Information Technology, which is the all-encompassing term for computers and communication and anything else that does not fit anywhere else.

1. When computing, whatever happens, behave as though you meant it to happen. Never show fear. Computers sense it and will then circle for the kill.

2. When you get to the point where your really understand your computer, then it's probably obsolete. Uncrated; outdated.

3. The first place to look for information is in the section of the manual where you least expect to find it. So look there before you look anywhere else.

4. When the going gets tough, the tough upgrade.

5. For every action there is an equal and opposite malfunction that tech support cannot understand. When the tech rep says "I never heard of that before," you are really in trouble.

6. To err is human...to really screw things up royally requires a computer. More than one computer can cause a disaster. An office full of computers could be the beginning of the end of life on this planet.

7. He who laughs last probably made a backup.

8. A complex system that does not work is invariably found to have evolved from a simpler system that worked just fine. We should never go beyond Version 1.0.

9. The Number 1 cause of computer problems is computer solutions.

10. A computer program will always do what you tell it to do, but rarely what you want it to do. So, tell it what you want it to do and hope it will be fooled.

A Stealth History of the World

Aristotle discovers the atom by staring
at a grain of sand.
Copernicus discovers with math and logic
that planets orbit the sun.
Galileo discovers gravity
without knowing what it is.
Newton discovers that light is matter.
Congress discovers that it can spend money it
does not have on planes that you cannot see to
fight an enemy that might not be there.

Computers in the future will go beyond small to chromosomal. Instead of silicon, data processing will be manufactured as DNA chains and inserted in human embryos. Input will come from optical character recognition and scanning with auditory conversion as well. The protoplasmic processor will apply the gigabytes of unused human memory cells. External memory options have not been determined; however, output will be via digital thought transference.

An expression in the year 2190 will be "Read my bits."

What you see is what you question: WYSIQUIZZICAL.

During an uncontrolled experiment on supplier invented a typesetter so fast that Futura was accidentally sent back in time. A 16th century printer saw it and exclaimed "That's grotesque." Hence our terminology.

In the next millennium there will be only one hyper intelligent font for all typography. You will specify any series of typographic characteristics, like "Give me a 17th century Dutch old style, with a larger x height, short ascenders and descenders, a swash version of the lowercase s, a two story lowercase g, and a hot metal look. And make it bold"

In the quest to eliminate direct sales organizations, one supplier is going to let you order a Chevy by dialing a 900 number, where upon $16,000 will be added to your phone bill. And you won't even get heavy breathing.

Now that the font wars have supposedly started, the Secretary of State has been engaging in shuttle diplomacy between Washington state and California. He is trying to limit the number of Scud missiles armed with Souvenir and get Bill Gates to give up the Golan Heights.
Why can't the entire airplane be made out of the same stuff the flight recorder is made of? Sure would be safer.

I am now at the ripe old age where Amtrak runs my train of thought, which is why I lose it so often.

A new dishwasher cleans ultrasonically. This a similar technology to that used in microwave ovens. Eventually, one unit could cook the food and clean the dishes. Then I'll cut out the middle man and the machine will cook, eat, clean, and electronically belch.

Went to buy a personal computer. The sales person asked "Shall I put it on your credit card? "No," I said "I really don't want one that small."

If the world is getting smaller, why are airfares going up?

Instead of a global village we may wind up with a global ghetto.

They're teaching chimps and porpoises to recognize icons. What's next, Shamu and a giant floating mouse?

There should be at least a seven day waiting period before you use Souvenir.

Actually, there is a 7-day waiting period before every 7-day waiting period.

The economy was so bad, Donald Trump laid himself off.

The Senate gave itself a pay raise in the middle of one night. This is what happens when the inmates run the asylum.

Money does not grow on tree, Automatic teller machines grow on trees.

Took a cruise to nowhere. It left me off in front of my house.

Between hardware and software, there is mushyware.

Moses may have been the first to use voice mail. Of course, it was followed by written confirmation.

I'm getting to the age where my train of thought needs a federal subsidy.

It's okay to use recycled paper, but not with recycled ideas.

One hospital guarantees that it will get you into the emergency room in 20 minutes. To accomplish this, they have sub-contracted ambulance service to Domino's Pizza. Appendectomy with anchovies?

"This is Frank Romano. My answering machine is not here right now, but if you will leave a message after the burp, it will get right back to you."

"This is Frank's answering machine. Frank is not here, but I am and have taken over."

We need another amendment to the Bill of Rights. Freedom of speech is not enough. We need a freedom to joke. Some people are taking humor too seriously.

First there was detent between Russia and the United States. Then East and West Germany remerged. Now, two superpowers reach agreement. Apple and IBM will work together on a new generation of workstations and systems. Meetings are scheduled in Geneva.

Where does this leave Microsoft? It is declaring its independence and seceding from the union. Slovenian troops have been seen in Redmond, Washington.

Even with Congressional scrutiny, NASA may finally get approval for the space station. However, Senator Byrd wants it in orbit over West Virginia.

Stealth Screening

Let's clear the confusion about halftone screening right now. The problem has to do with dots—not your run-of-the-mill dots but dots in shapes and sizes that stimulate levels of gray with black ink or toner. Even colors have levels of gray, which doesn't really make sense. These dots are then angled for each of the printing colors: yellow, magenta, cyan, black and electric turquoise to eliminate the problems caused by traditional printing presses.

Because of the way the dots overlap, we get what is known as moire, which results in yukky patterns running through your pictures.

The entire situation is now solved because of a revolutionary new technology called "stealth screening." (The patent application is blank and examiners are seeking prior art on emptiness.)

Stealth dots are perfectly round, but transparent. Thus, there is no need to angle them since if you angle a round dot, it rolls (the same is true if you oblique a bullet.) the dots are modulated by a wavelet astigmatism controlled by fuzzy logic that processes the pixels through a Cuisinart, using proprietary "slice and dice" technology. If this gets too technical refer to supplier literature or newsletter descriptions which are eminently clearer.

The dots are then colored individually by elves laid off from Santa's workshop in the summer (toys are now made in Taiwan.)

The elves use special stealth colors that are printed on a press that is run without any ink, which speeds makeready substantially. Since the images are not visible, moire is virtually eliminated, except for photos of snow on tinted paper.

At 400% magnification, you can see a lot more of nothing, which means that we may eventually develop stealth paper.

Still More Random Bits (Even)

With the experience Exxon has now had in removing gooey disgusting sludge from a wilderness landscape, they are ready to tackle the ultimate challenge: cleaning my teenaged son's room.

The only certainty is death and taxes. However, death is cheaper.

Conservatives want to go to Mars. Bon voyage. And take the liberals with you.

Why travel millions of miles to a desolate, hostile environment when you can get to the Bronx by subway.

Inferiority complex—if only the right people had one.

They have discovered the part of the brain that perceives color. It's the crayola cortex of the cerebellum.

Congress has decided to put nuclear missiles on trucks and the stealth bombers on hold.

We could always send Congress to Mars but then you can't fill a vacuum with a vacuum.

Congress really isn't so bad. It's the members that give it a poor name.

They say that it will take years to travel to Mars with stopovers on space stations and the moon. It's almost like taking Amtrak but I'll bet the food is better.

The argument for years was how many kerning pairs a system handled: 20, 100, 1400, 6000, infinity. Now the latest angels-on-the-head-of-a-pin debate is the number of dots per inch: 300, 400, 600, 900, 1200, 2540, 3000+. I say it's really how many dots you can kern.

What we have today is a group of high tech suppliers selling to a group of low tech users. This is the tech gap.

The United States of Microsoft

I guess the problem really started when Gates asked God to make Windows part of DNA. Something about a better human interface.

Poor Bill Gates. Somehow that's not the right adjective for the world's youngest billionaire.

If IBM and Apple ever merge, the new name will be WeBM.

Steve Jobs would then have his T-Shirts monogrammed.

Apple has AUX, its version of UNIX. IBM has AIX, its version of UNIX. Together they might have IXIX.

As you would expect, Microsoft wants MeNIX.

Why get angry with Microsoft because it's so big? IBM was big once.

What we have here is not David and Goliath, it's Goliath and Goliath.

I agree with Gates. His nuclear weapons are only for defensive purposes.

Apple is red. IBM is blue. Microsoft is green with envy.

Remember: Friends don't let friends set Souvenir.

Do you realize how many terms there are for computer-type people: propeller head, techie, hacker, machead, computer jockey, and nerd. Yet there is no term for someone who does not use a computer. Why not call computer users digital people and non-computer users analog people? I'm analog with digital tendencies.

After the events of the last few years, the only place where Communism may be allowed is in America.

IBM and Apple: a marriage of inconvenience for Bill Gates.

Remember The Mac OS called 7?

(Dated and apologies to Fred Astaire and "Cheek to Cheek.")

Seven, I'm in Seven
And my heart beats so
that I can scarcely scream
When seeking software System Seven clean
Seven, I'm in Seven
With a score of inits and cdevs
yet to be replaced
And most of my Mac programs
now a bloody waste
Seven, I'm in Seven
Waiting for revisions yet to come
Proving pioneering users can be really dumb
Seven, I'm in Seven
And my simple song is almost nearly done
As I sit and wait for System Seven Version 1.1.

Researchers at the National Institutes of Health have patented a method for simulating nerve impulses to the brain. This will lead to the invention of the artificial eye, or "very personal" scanner. The first versions were to be flat bed but the nose gets in the way.

Scanned a photo of myself and then ran the resultant image through OCR. Gosh, you can read me like a book.

In the movie Terminator III, Federal Express sends a cyborg his machine back in time to destroy the person responsible for FAX.

I was clicking across the TV channels when I stopped on C-SPAN, the service that broadcasts what little Congress does. There was this senator making an impassioned speech, rich with gesticulation and oratory. Then the camera went to a long shot and there was no one there. This poor soul was saying a lot about nothing to non-audience, to get his speech on the record, which no one would read.

Still having trouble making the conversion from type to color. I just tried to quad yellow.

Archaelogists have just discovered that ancient Israelites created scrolls on disks coded by light. The so-called Dead CD-ROMs used a crude code, now dubbed Aramaic ASCII. So far they only contain early recipes for sushi

Expert: Someone who understands everything about something, but can't explain any of it to anyone understandably.

A slow RIP is a DRIP.

The greatest lies
(like "The check is in the mail")

1. We'll catch any errors on the page proofs.
2. We'll do it desktop. It won't take long.
3. The printer can fix that in stripping.
4. The service bureau has the font.
5. Of course I sent the TIFF file.
6. The sales rep said so.

Sony has just announced a mini rewritable optical disk for audio recording. Someday these handy disks could be used for currency. Then the phrase "money talks" will have some real meaning. Money could even sing.

Paper tape and punch cards were optical storage media. You could see the holes. You could see through the holes.

Obit I Am
Dr. Seuss has died
Even the grinch cried

The only way to stop your subscription to *Modern Maturity* is to get younger.

A 4,000 year old Bronze Age man was found almost perfectly preserved in an Austrian glacier. He may be the ideal candidate for Director of the CIA, Supreme Court Justice, or Democratic Party presidential nominee.

If computers get too powerful, we can organize them into a committee—that will make them ineffective.

Progress

At a recent conference many speakers kept speaking about the progress of digital imaging, the progress of the industry, the progress of digital photography, the progress of electronic publishing. Here's my list of progressive and pithy platitudes.

Progress is 2% inspiration; 98% prevarication.

We should not confuse progress with machines or technology. New machines do not always move us ahead.

Progress comes from thinking deep thoughts, or just wondering about when lunch will be served.

Progress comes from impatience.

Progress never happens on weekends or postal holidays.

Progress is process, not a goal.

We are not making as much progress at progress as we have in the past, when progress was really progressive.

Progress is not really invention so much as rediscovery.

Progress only moves in one direction—but which one?

Progress only moves in one direction—the other one.

Progress is the impersistence of current technology.

Progress is okay, but it's gone on too long.

Progress is the inevitability of an idea whose time has come.

Progress should not be the embracing of what's new just because it's new.

Progress is never made by reasonable people. That's why I'm progressive.

Most of the real progress is made by mistake.

Columbus just happened to bump into a new world.

Real progress comes when you know when to eschew perfection. The laser printer is a good example.

A progressive is a liberal who knows where they're going.

Progress is about three minutes into the future.

A conservative progressive is retrogressive.

Progress is when you're going nowhere, fast.

Progress is a highway to Hades.

Progress is apparent after you get there, not while you're making the trip.

Build a better mousetrap and the world will beat a path to K-Mart.

Progress is seeing the world as it should be, not as it is.

The only thing wrong with progress is that we have to change everything to get it.

Getting older is not progress. Getting wiser is.

Progress is the future you envisioned yesterday, but didn't like when you woke up today.

Progress is not the future—it is the path to the future.

You do not make progress by paving the cow paths—you make progress by building the super highway.

If "con" is the opposite of "pro," then what is the opposite of progress?

Progress is what is ahead of us.

Type

Alexander Lawson defined typography as the perpetuation of a noble tradition.

One speaker told of hinting a glyph. I could only think of Jabberwocky: Twas brillig and the slithy glyph did gyre and gimble in the pixel.

They also spoke of scaling a bit map. My mind saw Sir Edmund Hillary at a press conference. "Why did you scale that bitmap?" Because it was there."

They are developing megafonts with very large character sets. This means that you will have to hold down the Control, Option, Shift, Tab and Escape keys while striking another key. This may require the Kama Sutra for fingers. But practice safe keyboarding.

Indigenous digits. I still don't know what they are. Sounds like a primitive group Margaret Mead once lived with.

I saw fonts for most known languages. And the New Adobe Multiple Master technology that can control both width and height and everything in between. This means that we can have people in remote parts of the world create bad type in more than one dimension.

Is there is a market for Multiple Master Mongolian.

Back in the old hot metal days, a kern was a swash part of a letter that over hanged (over hung?) another letter. Today this would be a glyph hanger.

Boy this industry is getting specialized. Just saw an ad for a single color separator. You get four negs but they're all the same color.

A new job description: some users call themselves "desk-toppers." But then so are blotters.

I'm writing a book. I've got the page numbers done.

What should we call users of PCs who create terrible looking pages for low res output? Naïve. What do you call users of PCs who create great looking pages? Professional.

I'm trying to hook up my Mac to a waxer. That way I won't feel guilty about still doing paste up.

In Memorial

Typography, Art of—Died recently and suddenly after being devoured by multiple predators in the destop environment. Typography, who never had any nickname on record, attained a certain celebrity status in the '70s and '80s, following the introduction of "The Godchild," otherwise known across the land as "cold type." Typography's health was known to have grown more delicate in recent years, although Typography's untimely death still came as a surprise, according to a family spokesperson. Another family member, however, reports that an apparent hereditary illness, said to eventually cripple its victims, has afflicted several close relatives. This includes twin first cousins, Syntax and Spelling. A sibling, Word Breaks, is reported institutionally insane. All are said to have been at one time closely involved in the family business and worked together quite harmoniously. Typography is survived, among others, by all the many brothers and sisters of the now-deceased Typesetting Services. Cash contributions accepted.

On the twelfth day of Christmas, my true love gave to me:

12 dashes dashing
11 daggars dueling
10 accents floating
9 parens enclosing
8 quotes a-quoting
7 slashes slashing
6 dipthongs dipping
5 bullets bouncing
4 dingbats dinging
3 ems a-spacing
2 super scripts
and a percent sign in a pi tray

What do I do for a living? I drag and drop.

What Will Replace Automation?

Human:
Human control and human energy.
Mechanization:
Human control and machine energy.
Automation:
Machine control and machine energy
Hyper automation:
Machines take the weekends off.

In the next millennium computers will mate. This gives new meaning to the terms "computer dating" and "chip off the old block." A new market for lawyers: computer divorce. Who will get possession of the PC Junior?

How to cushion the blow of new technology: use an air bag.

A blimp with an air bag is redundant.

A blimp is an air bag.

How about an air bag on a computer for system crashes?

Or how about an air bag for the stock market?

I put safety first, using a seat belt in a car with an air bag… and then never leave the garage.

My computer can now think and talk
Its scanner seems to always gawk
This may sound a bit absurd
I think I'll call it robo nerd

All things are relative: to a snail on the back of a turtle, the ride must be exhilarating.

Napoleon said that the old nobility would have survived if it had known enough to master printing. Of course, now they would have to master television or even the Internet. Control the means of mass communication and you have control. You have power.

Great minds discuss ideas. Average minds discuss events. Small minds discuss the *National Enquirer.*

To clean up oil spills genetic engineers have created a bug that eats oil. I once had a Volkswagen like that.

Met a unique liberal. He was generous with his own money.

The brohaha over flag burning and obscene lyrics has some folks calling for laws to limit our freedom of speech. It's like all those eastern European countries struggling for freedom. Their people never had the right to speak out in any form. And once they finally get their freedom, they will enact laws that take it away from themselves little by little.

The Hubble Space Telescope is really aligned properly. It's the universe that's out of focus.

So what if the Hubble Telescope blurs images. There is probably a market for a $1.5 billion kaleidoscope.

To rape the planet earth
Some people are intent
Now any day, the planet may
Return the compliment

Just received one of those sweepstakes letters from a weight loss clinic "You may already be thinner..."

I figured how to make my hard disk lose its memory; I lent it money.

The Germanys unite—a triumph of Deutsch marks over Karl Marx.

I think I've seen this all before
The feeling is not new
But I've seen it more than once
Is that déjà vu vu?

Robocop is a film about a household appliance with a gun. Robokerner intimidates letters into negative letterspacing.

Content versus Style

According to a research study, Macintosh users write at an 8th grader level and PC users writ at a 12th grade level. This was reported in Business Week. It seems that the Mac typographic format encourages a simple sentence structure (and perhaps some alliteration) with childish vocabulary. PC users are not distracted by form and therefore concentrate on content. When asked for a reaction, an Apple representative said simply "Goo."

Of all the items we have ever mentioned, the one that has generated the most reactions had to do with a *Business Week* blurb that reported Macintosh users wrote one or two grade levels below IBM PC (or clone) users. The original article appeared in *Academic Computing* in January, 1990. An English instructor at the University of Delaware noted that freshmen using Macs seemed to be turning in essays that were not as well written as those done on the PC.

Business Week ran the item in April and *TypeWorld* paraphrased it in May. Mac users were irate and claimed that there was no causal relationship between the machine and the person's ability. I disagree. When authors (writers, editors, etc.) deal with both form and content, there is a noticeable reduction in grammatical structure. It makes no difference if it is a mac or a PC—it is the preoccupation with format that diminishes attention to English detail.

That is why I recommend writing on a device that shows only typewriter characters on screen. We have not heard the last of this subject.

Random Bytes

They now have to distinguish between still video and motion video. What about moveable type? Is there stationary type?

Think of all the firms whose names end in X: Diconix, Autographx, Eikonix, Atex, ImagiTex, Camex, and Xerox. So far no one has used the name Xx—pronounced Zick-iks.

The UNIX Cheer
I nix
You nix
We all nix
For UNIX

Three engineers travel together in a car, one electrical engineer, one mechanical engineer, and one Microsoft engineer. After a long drive, the car suddenly breaks down with no obvious reason. The electrical engineer says "I don't know much about cars but let me check the electrical system, maybe I will find the problem."

The mechanical engineer says "I don't know much about cars but let me check the mechanical system, maybe I will fix it!"

The Microsoft engineer, who also wants to show some troubleshooting ability, says "I don't know much about cars, but why don't we close all the windows, get out, and get back in again."

Killer Viruses

News Item: The Pentagon is considering the use of "killer viruses to disrupt an enemy's use of computers. Honest.

Time: The near future.
Place: Aboard a magnetic medium with 144 members of the supersecret crack Commando Virus Team.

CV1: (his face covered with brown magnetic oxide camouflage). "We are almost at our destination and I can now reveal our mission. We are an elite team of electronic germ warfare specialists trained to create havoc in enemy computer systems."
CV2: "Does that make us Host Busters?"
CV1: "More than that, Private. You may have heard of the Dirty Dozen; we are the Gross Gross."
CV2:" Duck, here comes the read/write head again."
CV1: "We have our orders. Each of you occupy a different memory location an perform a single and disruptive action."
CV2: "Sarge, I don't like my orders. I signed on to see real action. It says here that I have replace all text in the active files with two whole weeks of the Congressional Record. Isn't that a war crime?"
CV3: "And I have to change all file names to Croatian curse words."
CV4: "That's nothing. I have to change all typefaces to Souvenir."
CV1: "You have all been trained for this mission. From boot camp where I took a motley crew of pre-protoplasmic recruits and molded them into a lean, mean microbe machine. We have our mission and we will perform it."
CV3: "Yeah, I remember when you taught us to read a bit map."
CV2: "And hide behind electronic spreadsheets."
CV3: "And counterfeit pixels."
CV4: "The read/write head is coming back."
CV2: "Get ready to jump."
CV3: "Lotus 1-2-3...Geronimo-o-o-o-o
CV1: "Fan out. Team 1 head for the CPU. Team 2 secure the disk drives. Team 3, come with me. We're going to hit the

read only memory. Rendezvous at 0400 at the serial port. Good luck, viri."

Time 0330, with Team 7 at the printer port
CV36: "OK, I've booby trapped the printer so that any page with more than four typerfaces will eject paper at Mach 2."
CV26: "Just received a message from Team 20. They are under heavy attack from a group on counterinsurgency pixels."
CV36: "Hop on the net and cover them."

Time: 0345, pinned down at the floppy drive:
CV67: "But it's never been used in virus warfare before. It is to data what anti-matter is to matter. It's information into a black hole."
CV55: "Fine one."
CV67: "It did it. They've been wiped out. But what will history say o us?"
CV55 "We came, we saw, we infected."

Time: 0400, at the RAM memory board:
CV1 "We lost 25 men but we accomplished our mission. This computer will never process anything intelligent again."
CV3: "Who does it belong to, Sarge?"
CV1 "Frank Romano."

Artificial Intelligence

My computer was programmed by a pseudo-intellectual with artificial intelligence and fuzzy logic—it works on the Federal budget.

A pseudo-intellectual is using an artificially intelligent machine: two dings don't make a bat.

Pseudo-intelligent machine: Radio Shack.

Pseudo-intelligent font: Souvenir.

The Personal Digital Assistant is an icon that looks like a person and seems to talk to you and takes your orders in future voice-based systems. Once again we are concealing the machine with a human façade.

A machine that acts like a person is a robot. A machine that looks and acts like a person is a cyborg. A person that acts like a machine is an automation. A person that looks and acts like a machine is a Marine drill instructor.

That's where real artificial intelligence should come in. Computers need not only No=0 and Yes = 1, but 0-1/2 = maybe.

Fuzzy logic is 0-1/2, mid-way between what is known and what is unknown.

Fuzzy logic is an infinite number of gradations of maybe.

Washington, DC is the fuzzy logic capital of the United States.

Computers may never emulate humanity because they do not feel pain or love or guilt. Artificial intelligence needs to be accompanied by artificial emotion.

When you put them all together, you have a system that knows what it doesn't know and everything in between. So if you can't be a pseudo-intellectual—fake it.

Pseudo-intellectuals say they know what they don't know. Artificial intelligence programs machines think they know what people know. Fuzzy logic is knowing but never being sure that you know, like Congress.

Futurists say that we will have a new generation of robots called knowbots. They will be programmed to think for you. Without having to work and without having to think, mankind is now ready to spend all of its time watching TV.

Artificial intelligence—we will know that it has arrived when one computer blames another computer. The result will be artificial arrogance.

We really need more organic intelligence, but it sounds like you're spreading manure.

Scientists now say that computers will eventually have animal-like traits. This means that they will be finicky about their input, claw the furniture, purr when they're contented, and require a litter box for data excrement.

The *New York Times* now reports on artificial reality, a concept introduced to the world by Al Gore. The *Times* says that a user wearing a special helmet that projects visual, auditory, and olfactory stimuli combined with special gloves that simulate tactile sensations result in the creation of a virtual world as perceived by the human subject but completely computer controlled. This venerable newspaper even reports that it would be possible to fake sexual experience, but this not a new idea. That kind of reporting will only lead to the next revelation: artificial journalism.

In the third millennium, when machines are in control, it will probably not be uncommon hear one of them complain that the "The person made a mistake."

Fuzzy Logic is a new branch of artificial intelligence that evolved because computers were too exact. This area deals with such inexact instructions as "Just a hair more." "Slightly left," "Just a smidgen," and "Reduce it down a little." Color separators still hear "Make it redder.'

What happens when artificial intelligence meets artificial reality? The *National Enquirer.*

The human brain is self-booting, multi-tasking computing system with voice, tactile, and visual recognition and high density random access memory. It is self-programming and utilizes real, rather than artificial, intelligence. This means that each of us is the ultimate personal computer.

Machines can never think. They have nothing to scratch, stroke, or puff on.

If machines can be programmed for artificial intelligence, they will they eventually develop mental aberrations, thus resulting in artificial paranoia. They would think that other machines were out to get them. They would then have both service technicians and computer (cyber) psychiatrists to take care of them

Computers are only human, but the opposite isn't so. If machines can have artificial intelligence, why can't people have artificial computer?

The newest utility program: an intelligence checker. You may be able to spell, but can you make sense?

Artificial artificial intelligence—where machines make the same mistakes that people make...like inventing machines that supposedly can't make mistakes.

People should think and machines should work. If you really watch what's going on, the machines are thinking and we're doing the work.

After artificial intelligence comes artificial religion. Your computer will forgive you for making an error.

First artificial sweetener now artificial fat. Add in artificial intelligence and you could have a bionic desktop publisher.

Stealth artificial intelligence. That's when you know less than nothing about something that does not exist.

If it weren't for people, how would we know that computers were smarter?

My computer is not smart enough to be artificially intelligent and not stupid enough to be a dumb terminal.

Artificial dumbness means that if the computer does think for itself, it's always wrong.

I've created artificial life and imbued it with artificial intelligence. I shall call it a TV sitcom producer.

Near artificial intelligence—like getting fully dressed, putting on a raincoat, and going out to flash nudists.

Artificial printout would 1000dpi but without the toner. Heck, since you can't see it anyway, go all the way to 6000dpi.

One computer I heard about has artificial hypochondria. It thinks that it has a virus.

My computer has artificial schizophrenia. It put venetian blinds on Windows.

Before you can achieve true artificial intelligence (as opposed to fake artificial intelligence) you must first reach superficial intelligence, a condition now monopolized by politicians, consultants, and those people on the Jerry Springer show.

The real danger of the computer age is not that computers will think like people but that people will think like computers. Where we were once afraid of being slaves, we must be wary of becoming robots.

What comes after artificial intelligence? Artificial wisdom. You know, like those pithy little gems you get inside fortune cookies.

There is a new form of societal elite forming in the computer world: the artificial intelligentsia.

So the commentator said that we were all familiar with artificial intelligence. He said that books and TV and movies were all examples of such unreality. He left out Congress and this book.

Some scientists believe that things inside their computers are actually alive. Of course, the real question is: what does it mean to be alive? Is a computer program alive? A computer virus can electronically reproduce; does that give it life? If you kill a virus program while it is being written, will Pro-Program-Lifers picket you?

Programs are said to be electronic versions of biologic entities and inhabit computer memory. Scientists want to use what they are calling artificial life to answer the question: how does nature create order out of chaos. It's easy, nature hires a management consultant.

We really do need artificial intelligence. There isn't enough of the real thing.

If a little knowledge is a dangerous thing, according to Alexander Pope, what is too much information? Trivial Pursuit.

You bring nothing into this world and you take nothing out of it. I forget if it was Saint Paul or E.F. Hutton who said that.

Random Bits and Bytes

Some day airlines will offer time travel. You can go to the future year 2090 to visit your progeny, but your luggage will wind up in the Middle Ages.

Massachusetts—where the budget may be balanced but the legislators aren't.

Actually, Mass politicians vote the same way they drive.

He is one of the most hated men in the world. His people live in fear of him; he attacks without mercy and is only concerned with victory, at any cost. Who is the tyrant? Saddam Hussein of Iraq? Mummar Quadaffi of Libya? No, George Steinbrenner of baseball's Yankees.

A microchip maker that I know has been so successful it has expanded my moving into smaller quarters.

A planned protest by United Airlines was delayed when the picket signs were shipped to the wrong airports.

You send a fax. The recipient makes a note on it and faxes it back to you. This is a copy of a fax, which is really a transmitted copy. You then make a note on it and re-fax it. This is a copy of a copy of a fax copy. The recipient copies the sheet on a copier, which makes it a copy of copy of copy of a fax copy. What do you call any level of copying beyond this? Unreadable.

In a reciprocal agreement, McDonalds was allowed to open a store in Moscow and a Russian firm will open a store in Manhattan. Of course, the shelves in the latter will be empty.

Genetics engineers have discovered that maleness is determined by a special Y chromosome. Not just any Y chromosome. It must be a Garamond Bold Italic small cap Y.

Astrophysicists have found a gap in the rings of Saturn. Former president Clinton immediately issued a denial.

Work of art: that which the public takes no interest in until it is attacked as obscene.

I was at a party that was so trendy, no one arrived until everyone else had.

With a lifetime of typography behind me, I'm having difficulty getting the hang of color. The other day I tried to kern magenta and cyan.

The speaker described the ultra high speed networks of the future as "data super highways." I could only picture micro data troopers on pixel cycles pulling speeding bits over for exceeding the mips limit.

I can't afford a car phone so I bought the cheaper version: two tin cans and a cellular string.

1960s
God is dead
1980s
Elvis is alive
2000s
Computers are human

My answering machine answered one of those computer calls. Now it's going steady with the computer.

A committee is a group
Doing the work of one
A secretary is one
Who sees that the work gets done.

Just say "no' to a negative attitude.

There are 40 million Nintendo games out there. We are told that the kids who use them will determine the future of electronic information systems and technology. However, they will need a joy stick to read the news on computer screens.

I'd explain it to you, but your brain might explode.

Went to a Macintosh extravaganza the other day. The audience of Mac users has matured. Many of the attendees were wearing suits and ties. They still wore sneakers, but they did have suits and ties.

There is a corner of our front yard where the grass never had a chance to grow. The kids played there with Tonka trucks as they built imaginary highways and cities. The rode their Big Wheels and two-wheelers and played ball with the immediate world. When they started driving, they could never quite make the turn into the driveway, leaving ruts in the ground, crushing any blade of grass that might grow. Yesterday the second of our sons went off to build his own life. I stared out the window and saw that little corner of the yard, now green and plush...and silent.

Can you have multimedia on a monochome monitor with a single tasking system?

Multimedia may let you have a new key on the computer keyboard that says "Tell me more." I want it to "Tell me why?"

Good decisions
come from knowledge.
Knowledge
comes from experience.
Experience
comes from bad decisions.

Of course, after multimedia comes multi-dimensional media. You can produce documents that let you go inside them. Cyber pages if you will. Smarter than smart paper. I can picture someone, someday, trapped inside a memo and being bored to death.

You can get inside a word or become part of a picture. No longer will they say "Jim has a presentation;" they will say "Jim is the presentation."

You open a book and a person's face appears, reading to you. Each page is LCD array and softspeaker (the opposite of a loudspeaker). You ask it questions and it answer you in whatever language you use. Your turn to another page and it becomes a video that displays motion, in color of course Your converse with Plato and listen to Bach play his own music. Eventually, you visit unknown places and walk the streets. You go inside and atom and outside the universe. You travel through time and space. It is the real computer age. You have become data.

The Artificial Man. The story of a bio-engineered protoplasmic entity imbued with pseudo intelligence and average abilities, attempting to scale the heights of mediocrity. Just call him George.

So far I have seen magazine inserts with odors, holographic images in three dimensions, and some that play music when you open them. Pretty soon you open *Time* and find a princess standing there hawking Obi Wan cologne.

Operating Manual Pills. Just pop one in your mouth and learn a program instantly. Danger! Do not take more than one at a time or you will know too much for your own good.

The Year is 2190 and You are There...

The Postal Service, now a subsidiary of UPS, assigns a 13-digit Zip code to every human being on earth, This allows for direct addressing via personal satellite dishes which are worn by most people in place of hats.

Actually, phones have been made chromosomal. You just think of the person you want to call and you are connected with that person, no matter where they are. There is no such thing as a wrong number; it is now a wrong person. A busy signal means the person is busy.

Anti-magnetic hover craft clog the skies at rush hour. Traffic watches are now on the ground, looking up. Accidents are called crack downs.

Wrist-worn workstations are commonplace with voice communication or voice-to-print conversion. If you sneeze into the microphone, the printer prints four pages of s's.

Sub-atomic electronics results in sub-micro-miniature computer technology. Computers are more that personal; they are intimate.

Consumers start a new trend by demanding printed versions of their audio and video cassettes. Retail operations arise to sell manually processed media. They are called bookstores.

Computers have been programmed with a survival instinct, often blaming people for errors and sending sarcastic memos.

Monetary and credit transactions are via retinal eye scan. Patrons in restaurants still tear up small sheets of carbon paper as a ceremonial ritual. No one remembers why.

Tanning salons have been replaced by instant replay parlors where you can re-live memory experiences. Those in arrears have their memories replaced by those of Pee Wee Herman.

The Supreme Court is made up of eight women and one (token) man. He objects to chiffon robes.

Congress still cannot decide what to do about the deficit.

A humungabyte is a trillion trillion bytes of data storage, about the size of a 1990's dime. It still cannot hold a year's worth of the Congressional Record.

Digital images are now holograms, projecting computer images of reality on demand. Lonely people go steady with inflatable holograms.

The Census Bureau now counts people from satellite sensors in outer space by reducing them to pixels. However, everyone on the planet must stand still for three minutes.

I called the computer to check on the error in my bill. It said the person did it.

An apple a day
Covered in chemical spray
Certainly keeps the doctor away

It has just been discovered that the hold in the Ozone layer is directly over the U.S. Capitol.

Money Talks; Mine Mumbles

The *Wall Street Journal*, one of the most prestigious newspapers in the world, reports a shortage of mouseballs. You know, those little balls inside your computer mouse. The world faces major economic problems and the *WSJ* worries about mouseballs.

Scientists are searching for signs of artificial intelligence in the universe.

So far every state now states that it's population was understated. Where did all those missing people go? Now it can be revealed. Under a top secret military program stealth people were surreptitiously introduced into the population. Remember the hippies for the Sixties? Seen any lately? Noticed that the yuppies are gone? Seen a liberal Democrat of late? Stealth people were created for PR purposes, but budget cuts have reduced their number and only a few remain, like Jerry Brown and Newt Gingrich.

I had this feeling I never had before
I saw something I never ever saw
There was just one last thing I could say
This was a case of vuja dé

We should send our troops where they are really needed: New York City. Can you imagine metropolitan taxi drivers using urban (yellow) tanks? You get in and the driver says "Where to?" To annex Jersey City!"

Hypertext. Cure: electronic valium.

Q: Where will the industry be in 2010?
A: Peoria. It's as good an answer as any.

The oil situation has become so acute Exxon may soon have to spill oil from its reserves.

Oil keeps going up in cost and computer memory keeps going down. What we need is a car that is fueled by computer chips. Like "Filler up with 128k of dynamic RAM.

I have been using the term "ransom note publishing' to describe the poor use of type by many desktop users. Now there is a need for term to describe the poor use of color:

1. Jackson Pollack on a bad day.
2. An explosion at Sherwin Williams.
3. Meltdown at Crayola Crayons.

I don't have an attitude problem. You have a perception problem.

I love deadlines. I especially like the whooshing sound they make as they go flying by.

Two wrongs don't make a right, but three rights make a left.

I'm not just a gardener, I'm a Plant Manager.

On the keyboard of life, always keep one finger near the Escape key.

Mind Links will require a new form of message dialing. You just think of someone's address and be connected. Will there be busy signals if they are mindlinking already. If there is no answer the party is dead. For privacy you can get an unlisted mind. You are now the ultimate mobile phone. Just think—no more annoying cell phone beeps.

Color

It is Fall in new England and the leaves have turned to bright gold and red and all the colors in-between, so I'm feeling colorful.

The *USA Today* weather map says that tomorrow will be yellow with a touch of red in the Northeast.

Psychologists say that we dream in color. Your can sharpen the image by dreaming of a test pattern. Is that dream RGB or CMYK?

After age forty males lose color perception. Sort of tonal impotence.

One color is worth a thousand words, like the red of an autumn sunset.

One word is worth a thousand colors, like fireworks on the 4th of July.

Black is the absence of color; white is all colors. Plaid is not a color.

The sky is blue, the grass is green
Words can't express the color I mean
How blue is blue? How green is green?
From light to dark and shades between
Colors are described by fools like me
Instead by Pantone, Numerically

You can remember the colors of the spectrum by knowing ROY G BIV—red, orange, yellow, green, blue, indigo, violet. Backwards it's VIB G YOR.

Actually you cannot see color with your eyes closed or in the dark. There is only the memory of color, like grass or sky. Color is the perception or reflection. If there is no light, there is no color. Color is what you think it is.

Color or colour. It's up to u.

A Brief History of Color

Adam and Eve were actually black and white. It was only after the apple episode that the world became color. If mankind was to live in sin, it might as well do it with a little style.

Colors did not have names until an Egyptian slave, Ptolemy Pturner, wrote an ode to King Tut and needed a word to rhyme with "you." During the Dark Ages bright colors were banned by the Church, which led to underground trading of color swatches wrapped in plain brown paper.

Galileo tried to measure the speed of light by dropping both a small and a large candle from the leaning Tower of Pisa. The result was a waxy buildup. Later Newton discovered that light caused color or that light was color when a candelabra fell on his head.

Color radio was introduced in the Twenties but did not catch on until someone thought to use a video screen.

Déja blue: That cyan seems familiar.

Desktop color is better that it looks.

Manet or Monet,
I can never be right
About impressionist painters
who color with light
They all seem to blend
into contrast and hue
But I've seen them before;
is that Dégas vu?

Saw one of those color publishing systems that let you electronically retouch color pictures. They took a photo of the U.S. Capitol, framed through a bough of cherry blossoms, and modified it. They put more cherry blossoms on the branches by cloning them, but they couldn't put more conservatives in Congress. Too much cloning perhaps. The liberals already had their pixels re-pointed.

No Random Bits Here

Went to MIT's time-space lab. Got lost and had to refer to one of those locator maps. It said "You are here" but it was a map of the Milky Way.

Bumped into Lee Iacococa at a meeting recently. Fortunately he was equipped with an air bag.

Megahertz: a very large car rental organization.

If you want to really show how advanced you are, you could have an answering machine attached to your car phone that says you're not in because you're home.

I stayed at a really cheap conference hotel recently. They sent a wake-up memo.

You can now get an infrared cordless mouse. I'd prefer a mouseless cord.

A desktop counterfeiter got caught because they reversed the front and back of a $20 bill.

Smile of the week: As useless as an ATM at a sperm bank.

It is now possible to create Century Expanded Condensed Bold Outline Drop Shadow Oblique Small Caps Superscript in Pantone 352.

I bought a model Amtrak train set for a Christmas gift. It arrives December 26th.

How to fix the Hubble Space Telescope: Windex.

There really is evolution as Darwin said. It just hasn't happened yet.

Decision: what you are forced to make if you can't get a committee together.

I'm feeling kinda user friendly.

One meeting I went to was so boring I fell asleep in the middle of my nap.

If you microwave a digital watch on ultra high you can send time back in time.

There are more people alive today than the sum total of all people who ever lived and died before. And they all like to take drives on weekends and go shopping at exactly the same time I do.

Microgears are 30 microns in size and can be assembled into micro gear boxes that are driven by teeny tiny motors to run microscopic robots to fix itsy bitsy machines. And you think you have trouble finding your tools—how about a subatomic allen wrench?

How come they never have a layoff in Congress?

If the oil situation exacerbates, Exxon may have to spill oil from the Strategic Petroleum Reserve.

A disk array is group of disk drives linked together like Christmas tree lights. You have to tighten each one before you can use them.

Most-interesting-product-department: electric paint. It generates heat when voltage is passed through it. This could lead to electric graffiti, like "The Lord saves, but Moses invests…in Internet stocks." It also means that if you paint the walls, ceiling, and floors you could steam cook someone in their room. A room-sized microwave. This could wipe out the market for electric blankets. Just coat your body with the magic paint and stick a finger in a socket.

A new form of disk drive uses glass disks. The glass platter is coated with metal oxide instead of aluminum. High density versions will be made out of crystal.

A while back the space shuttle had to fix a broken drain while orbiting the earth. Where did they find a plumber on a weekend? Who makes outer space calls?

NASA is being sued by the makers of the Yugo automobile who say that the space shuttle copies their design.

The automobile and the telephone are the most popular "technologies" that people has mastered. That makes a mobile phone almost mandatory. A telephone booth on wheels. Eventually you could be pulled over for talking too fast.

They're working on a VCR that's programmed by voice. It must be an foreign voice.

I'm hiring a consultant to program my VCR.

Some VCR's come with a video tape instead of an instruction manual. How do you figure out how to play the tape to figure out how to play the tape?

How will civilization end? The last VCR on earth will blink the last 12:00 AM and fade into darkness.

Smaller is not always friendlier, although it does not apply to kittens. They are always friendly.

Newspapers now print a code in the TV listings to automate the taping of certain shows at certain times. Eventually, TV shows will flash codes to tell you which printed publication articles to read and copy.

Some folks are so lazy they have a remote control for their TV remote control so they don't have to get up to get the remote control.

"Now this model has 80 megabytes of RAM and 100 gigabytes of disk storage with 24X CD- and DVD-ROM plus RISC processing..."
"How much is it?"
"$2,200."
"Isn't that a little high for a toaster?"

Phones aren't that simple. I have a model with 22 extra buttons. I can transfer calls to my heating pad.

How about the friendly key sequence for one of the desktop programs: hold down an Option and Shift while depressing Command and Tab during a mouse click but before a Return on the third Friday after a full moon.

I once complained because the keys on a keyboard were too close together. The manufacturer said that my fingers were too far apart.

It's called invisible technology. Computers are hidden so that only the screen is visible. Soon the screens will be invisible and images will be projected. That will give us screenless screens, keyless keyboards, and computerless computers. But you will need a plugable electrical plug.

Computer euphemisms

1. He's running on only 1K of RAM
2. His CD-ROM is scratched.
3. Not playing with a full disk.
4. His mental MIPS is a negative.
5. All stop bits and no parity
6. He's got a megabyte of zeros
7. Wake up and scan the pixels.
8. He has a Write Only Memory.
9. He gives old meaning to the term SCSI.
10. He can only Lotus 1-2
11. He has blurry Windows.
12. His read/write head is permanently parked.

It's not true that computer viruses are caused by computer dating.

Actually, I got a virus the same day my PC did, but the PC had protection and I did not. So I wound up with the flu. What this country needs is personal virus protection; it immediately shuts your mouth, seals your nose, and plugs you ears. You are now locked and are now protected against any virus entry. And probably dead.

I read that scientists are working on artificially intelligent microbes, sort of AI DNA. Just what we need, a generation of smart germs. The dumb ones were bad enough.

The secret weapon in the Persian Gulf has just leaked out: a stealth camel.

The very notion of an electronic brain is ludicrous. At my age, an electronic kidney would be better.

The micro boom has finally reached the Bible. They have put the Old and New Testament in one 4-ounce computer with LED screen and keyboard. You can search for verses, etc. I intend to carry one in my pocket all the time. You never know when you might be hit by an electronic bullet.

I'm getting tired of WYSIWYG. Is that WEARYWIG?

A History of Computer Portability

1960 Mainframe
1970 Mini
1980 Desktop
1981 Luggable
1984 Portable
1986 Laptop
1190 Notebook
1995 Palmtop
2000 Implant
2006 Genetic

My machine is artificially evasive—it avoids making decisions.

Just read that scientists are trying to develop a strain of cotton that can grow in color. They decided on white with paisley fleurs-de-lis.

An Ode

Where do computers
Ultimately go to die?
They all wind up I imagine in
A graveyard in the sky.
There you'll find the Osborne
And the Apple Lisa, too.
The Kaypro and Commodore,
And the Jr. from Big Blue.
Some are running MS DOS
And some run CP/M
With Visicalc and Wordstar
And even G-E-M.
Some are in their glory
For serving us so well.
And others bomb forever
In a place called PC hell.

Microsoft has a pet name for Windows. Fido? No...

They call it OS-Me-Too.

The singing document. A speaker said that documents of the future would be accompanied by sound. Since music is sound, you could go way beyond boldface and emphasize your points with some Bach or Wagner.

What did nerds do before computers?

Tombstone typo: a grave error.

Some problems are so complex it takes a higher form of intelligence (artificial or otherwise) just to be confused about them.

Computers have lots of memory but no imagination.

Mixed emotions: I shipped my modem by Federal Express.

We often mistake slogans for solutions.

Contradictions: a militant peace activist.

Seeing color on the screen requires a new acronym: CWYSI-WYG.

To err is human, thus erasers have pencils.

The economy is getting to the point where lobbyists are laying off Congressmen.

CNN recently interrupted a special news bulletin with a regularly scheduled program.

On Amtrak, when you order milk, there are pictures of lost passengers on the container.

Creative marketing: a combined donut shop and weight loss clinic.

My voice mail system is ill; it has laryngitis.

Is a consultant who insults your intelligence an "insultant"?

Some people suffer from mental graffiti.

Megalithic and disorganized companies remind us of the reason that dinosaurs are extinct: large bodies with brains the size of a pea.

The B1 Bomber required one million pages of documentation. Why don't we drop all that paper on the bad guys instead of nasty bombs? In fact, many of the memos of American industry could bore our enemies to death—sort of neutron correspondence.

An exhibition of desktop publishing products was dubbed the "vaporware fair." Remember "blue sky" as a euphemism for "not practical," "out of this world"—well now we have another one. The term must be used to refer to products that are still being developed. Of course, this never stopped sellers from selling…and buyers from buying.

A play in four acts: Act 1: A firm realizes it needs a computer. Act 2: A committee is appointed, which travels from supplier to supplier. Act 3: Each supplier emphasizes capabilities that it has unique from its competitors. Act 4: The committee duly notes each feature and writes a specification that incorporates all these unique features—for a system that no supplier can supply. Moral: got me?

The opposite of "mousing an icon" is "pucking a palette."

At the recent show, our booth was visited by many attendees who asked how to get to desktop publishing. "Lose your way, your intelligence and your standards," we directed.

Saw a great Apple commercial a while back. It showed Gutenberg trying to plug a Macintosh cable into his printing press. Now that Apple has hired old Johann and Xerox once had Leonard DaVinci under contract (they are now into Olympian gods), I have decided to represent historical personages for industry suppliers. I'm having difficulty finding work for Ivan the Terrible (a pussycat, actually) and Innocent III (popes are people too). The Invisible Man has signed on to represent Data General because no one has seen them lately.

This is the only industry where suppliers introduce products that do not exist...which are purchased by firms that do not have the money.

Sat in on a seminar the other day where a speaker wanted to describe a device as "ergonomically designed" but called it "anatomically correct." The first desktop system with genitalia?

Now that there's Computer Town and Computer City, I'm starting Computer Ghetto for really cheap PCs. They come in a brown paper bag.

Sam and The Computer

Sam lost everything in the computer today...again. The first time he was fooling around with the various disk operating system commands and keyed ERASE*.* which erased everything. That wasn't too bad since only a few programs were resident on the 10Mb rigid disk at the time. (Boy, is this dated.)

Today he tried to format a floppy, which is the "A" drive, but didn't notice that he was still in the "C" or rigid disk drive. The computer faithfully carried out the command and formatted the rigid disk, thereby destroying the data stored thereon.

This time Sam had set up a rather intricate accounting program with a large master file. He can reload the program but the file will be re-keyed (by Sam).

He was smiling I should note, but deep in his heart computers have certainly received another black mark for being so stupid as to wipe out everything.

We decided that this error should not have been committed in vain if it might be instructive and help another soul lost in the morass of personal or other computer. We are all in this together.

The first lesson to be learned has to do with those machine functions that can erase or change data. Learn them first and know the exact use of them. Computers are unforgiving. If you type the wrong character, it won' know.

The next lesson has to do with backup. Sam just went out and bought five boxes of floppies to backup the rigid disk. Keying and re-keying are not his strong suit.

No one ever told us when we got the computers, "Don't do this or you'll wipe out everything." It's not their fault. The manual says that will erase everything with *.* (and it assumes that you would use it accordingly). Manuals assume too much.

After all these years in typesetting Sam and I can warn you about typesetting problems because we have made them all. Now, like many of you, we are learning from our PC mistakes. Good luck.

We'll all need it.

At an imaging conference I learned that in the world of visual perception, things that are viewed differently are different and things that are viewed the same are also different. To make things visually the same, they must be made different, because we look but we do not see and we see but we do not notice. Reality is only that which is perceived and perception is imprecise. I haven't the faintest idea what I just said but three scientists and two PhDs said I'm right.

Deconstruction is the name given to a way of thinking that says that we never mean what we say and that words don't say what we really mean. Reading is said to be subjective and each reader brings to the process a personal filter based on their experience, education, etc. What we find in a text is affected by other texts and vice versa. Language is not a tool, but a force that acts through each of us. The dictionary is therefore obsolete since words are defined in terms of other words whose meanings are suspect. Communication undermines any attempt to impose order upon it. This philosophy is especially appropriate for consultants.

My Computer Hates Me

I purchased a Bernoulli Box backup disk unit from Iomega and noticed an 800 number for problems printed in the manual. For the heck of it I called the number to see how thy handled problems. The call was answered by a recording that told me to contact my dealer. Why didn't they just say than in the manual?

The cyberphobe has fear of computers. A kernophobe fears close relationships.

All kinds of rumors are flying about both. Apple and IBM introductions that are supposedly imminent. So here's ours" IBM and Apple will merge to form ABM and the logo will be a blue kumquat. Then, George Soros will attempt a hostile takeover and Allied-Signal will appear as a white knight. Eventually all firms will be a part of AOL and no one will recall what desktop publishing was.

The French Foreign Legion just bought a computer and programmed it to forget. Memory capacity is minus three megabytes.

It's amazing what some vendors call a system. Just hook up a variety of devices and you supposedly have one. Single units are now called systems because they have multiple components. I guess a hammer is a nail driving system.

If you play with hardware long enough, it breaks. If you play with software long enough, it works. In between, just do it long enough to require eyeglasses.

Now the Ross Perot has invested in NeXT, Inc. can we expect him to rescue hostages from the hot tubs of Marin County? (OK, it's old news, but I like it.)

People who are addicted to video terminals are called tube junkies.

Now there's a vaporware creation program. It lets you create a non-working demonstration version of a planned product that does not exist in order to raise money and garner trade interest.

Just heard about dribbleware—software that dribbles out a little at a time. Dribble software is a phased release of non-existing programs. Sort of like most TV fare.

Wait until Xerox learns that Zeus has just switched to IBM. Something about script control.

Computers can do more that people because they never have to stop and answer the phone.

The two-volume Oxford English Dictionary makes an ideal rotatable stand for the Macintosh screen.

Steve Jobs told the assemblage that the PC has peaked; that the Mac has also peaked. Actually, Steve Jobs has peaked.

Some of the programs being exhibited could give vaporware a bad name.

Some of the talk sounded like a commodities exchange:

"I need a 286 with EGA and 40 meg."

"How about the 286 with CGA and 20 meg?"

"Can I get Model 5 with hydraquadder and last mat kicker?"

Multitasking: the ability to do several things badly at the same time.

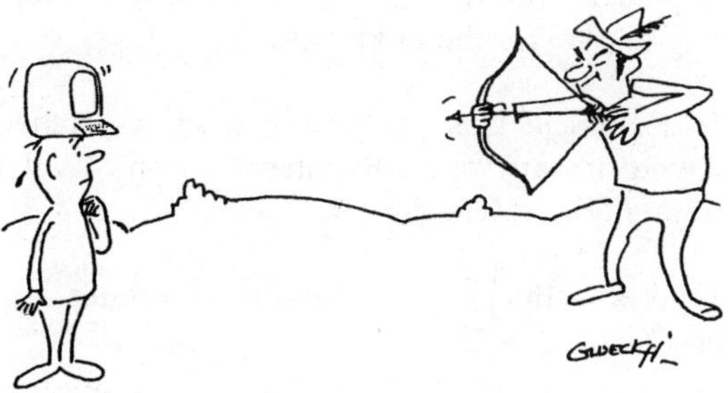

The *Wall Street Journal* had an article recently on how the optical disk was finally going to create the paperless office. When the *WSJ* itself goes to optical disk, then I'll believe it.

Was at a seminar presented by a group of tech-no-nerds (you know, pocket protectors with seventeen different colored pens) who were talking about laser positioning systems. If the polygon mirrors do not rotate perfectly you get wobbling rasters. All I could thin of was Elmer Fudd telling of wobbling wasters the wesult of wascally wabbits. So much for a college education.

Just bought an impersonal computer. Turn it on and it ignores you.

Why can't a PC be as reliable as a mainframe, the DP manager asked, citing 99.9% uptime for the big computer. Well, if you put each PC in a glass room, with special power filters, special environment and sanitized people, you might be able to get that level of reliability.

Ever notice how the light that emanates from under the copier cover looks like a scene from Friday the 13th part 78.

The period between the installation of your new machine and the end of the warranty period is hypertime

Market research people are like to psychics who write predictions for the *National Enquirer.* Neither has to be right, Just ambiguous and tittilating.

Market research: predicting the unpredictable for the unknowing to plan for the unknown.

The Delphic Oracle was the first market researcher. Its answers were always open to interpretation. "Will I be king?" You will be crowned."

A Los Angeles technocrat: "Have your computer call my computer..."

Prayer is a toll-free call.

As one of those people who made the transition from Royal manual typewriter to IBM Selectric to Redactron word processor to PC, I am asked what I prefer. I prefer dictating to another person.

There's junk mail...will we have junk fax? And junk e-mail?

Wang (remember them?) once ran radio and TV ads that spouted inside computer jargon, like "I checked the REP for SNA on the LAN for MIS." If data processing people really do talk like this, it's easy to understand why there are locks on computer room doors. And they may not be there to keep people out...

Best line of a recent conference: "I came because I was confused and when I left, I was confused on a higher level."

My favorite error message is "An irrecoverable error has occurred and all data on your rigid disk will be lost. OK" I don't want OK; I want "*#$you." I want some ancient Persian course. I want to inflict harm. I want revenge. OK, OK, I'm better now.

It was one of those exclusive clubs where wealth goes to admire itself. A patrician gentleman was overheard pontificating; "When will society be prepared for the digitization of all knowledge?" Actually, we could reduce the memory requirement significantly by only storing all that society has actually learned. One punch card would be more than adequate.

Y2KMart is Cheap Chic

If you think about it, facsimile transmission is just an early version of the Star Trek transporter. Today, pages; tomorrow, "beam me up, Scotty." You could expand or condense yourself by modifying protoplasmic rasters. You could italicize yourself. Your could store friends on disk. Air travel would be eliminated. However, static on transmission lines could result in your looking like Quasimodo.

Secondhand nodes, my net has secondhand nodes.

Vignette: As usual, I was on an Amtrak train riding from New York to Boston recently and the guy next to me in the Club Car had and IBM portable PC which he was clicketty-clicking to death. Then just when I thought I would get some quiet he whips out a cellular telephone and proceeds to call most of the population of Cleveland.

After that, he went at a calculator that looked like an old IBM 1620. By New Haven, he was joined by others and they moved a few seats away to have a business meeting. This was interesting to me since I like trains because they get me away from computers, telephones, meetings, etc.

One year, during a snowstorm I was next to a businessman who couldn't get a flight so settled for the train. After a long period of staring out the windows he said, "I never noticed the trees before."

Just read an article on ergonomic mouses (Honest). Magazines have to put something in between the ads.

I've seen it all department: electric socks. They're battery operated to keep your feet warm. They could lead to an entire line of electronic clothing…like gloves that double as digital input devices or binocular nose-mounted video screens.

Stealth vaporware consists of non-existent non-working programs that turn your protoplasm to Silly Putty without affecting your Reeboks.

Q: Why did the dinosaurs disappear?
A: They sat at video terminals all day long.
Heck, we blame everything else on terminals.

I can't decide whether to invest in fine wine, gold coins, postage stamps or DRAM computer chips.

A new training aid: "Operating Manual Tablets"—just pop one in your mouth and learn a program instantly. Danger, do not overdose or you will suffer from over-smartness.

Saw two articles recently about computers. One mentioned super minicomputers and the other talked about mini supercomputers. I then learned that there are mini micros and micro minis and perhaps micromicros. Next thing you know we'll have liberal and conservative computers. A middle of the road unit would be a midi mini.

[Name your company] has just undergone another corporate reorganization. Some feel it may be a re-dis-organization. Apple has applied for copyright protection on the look and feel of corporate reorganizations, but once again, they have been beaten by Xerox. General Motors, of course, holds the world's record for the number of reorganizations in a single day. Re-organizations do not really change anything, but management always feels that they are actually accomplishing something.

The consultant's credo: I came. I saw. I confused.

Q: How many consultants does it take to change a light bulb?
A: None. They can only predict a billion dollar market for light bulbs

So the patient asked the psychiatrist, "Should I go Windows or Macintosh?" "It depends," he said.. "Which would you recommend?" the patient continued. "Well how do you feel about it?" "I like Windows because there's so much of it around but Macintosh is more innovative. What's best for me? "What do you think is best for you?" "I'm not sure...I sort of lean toward Windows...and Macintosh. I'm confused" "Does that concern you?'

"Yes, I'm a consultant."

If you offer some consultants a penny for their thoughts it's probably a pretty fair value.

After desktop publishing comes the more portable "pocket publishing." You can buy it at K-Mart.

Twenty years ago my eyes were sharp and the video screens were fuzzy. Now it's the other way around.

I sat down at the PC to edit, layout and produce a book. So I prayed for the strength to get the job done. Then I packed it up and sent it to the production department. God sent me wisdom instead.

I'm working on a series of bubble gum cards of famous typefaces. Collect the entire set.

Time flies—and no frequent flyer discount. The inadequacies of some programs give you WYSIWYD—What You See Is What You Deserve.

How do you compare a TV evangelist to desktop publishing. One tells you how good it will be if you're not bad and the other tells you how good it will be if you are bad. I don't know which is which though.

Aerial publishing is skywriting; personal publishing is really tattooing.

I sat for two days at a seminar in which about twenty speakers used the terms spots, dots, pels and pixels—and no two used them the same way.

There is no truth to the rumor that some desktop publishing programs will be shipped with a supply of Prozac.

I visited a firm the other day that was having a problem with personnel turnover. The management asked me which technology would eliminate people—nuclear weapons, I replied.

Do you get the feeling that the *Enquirer* and *Star* have brought everyone to their level? I believe that I am the offspring of alien beings—would a normal person write stuff like this?

Have you heard the other Wang ads offering jargon-rich war stories? Here's another version: "I was on the 11 a.m. Metroliner out of DC sitting next to Leonardo DaVinci. According to him anyone with a pica ruler and a non-repro blue pen is into corporate publishing. I told him Wang had linked the VS to SPS over a net with lots of mips and a low cost per seat. With servers everywhere emulating SNA and no IBM iron. Then he asked me if we could hook up tow Model 5s and in Elrod. I told him to stop using arcane terminology."

Computers have gone from mainframe to mini to desktop to laptop to palmtop. Coming soon: fingertip top.

If you backslant the typeface Eras you can straighten it out. By the way, if you oblique a bullet, does it roll?

What do the budge deficit, the trade imbalance and desktop publishing have in common? Too much out, not enough in, too much in, not enough out, and not much is enough.

What's a synonym for thesaurus?

Romano's Law #375: The fancier the seminar promotion, the less value there is to the seminar.

Pat Werner Mintz, one of our favorite industry writers, just dropped a note: "I've given up graphic arts for historical romances." The accompanying promotion from PaperJacks was for a book called "Timbers and Gold Lace"—"One woman fights for her life and love to overcome destiny's challenge." Therefore I've decided to dust off one my old ideas for a novel: "Desktop Lust"—heck, we do everything else on it.

Baloney has a million uses. Sliced, it's used in sandwiches. Chopped, it's used in salads. Printed, it's used in electronic publishing promotions.

Saw a promo for a printer that claims "near typeset quality." Near what? Near dot matrix quality is probably one dot to the inch.

Great product idea: a combination desktop publishing system and paper shredder for government use.

I'm working on a line of toy dolls called Cabbage Patch Publishers.

People should think and machines should work. If you watch what is going on, the machines are thinking and we are doing all the work.

OK, who's the wiseguy? I received a package labeled "The Ultimate Desktop Publisher. Does anything you want it to do." Inside was a sheet of transfer type and a burnisher.

One country's military wants a laser printer that would survive a nuclear blast. That's so they can produce manuals on how to fight with sticks and stones.

Typographic Politics. Democrats set their line fast and loose; Republicans set them slow and tight. Democrats are Ragged Left; Republicans are Ragged Right. Democrats us Avant Garde; Republicans use anything with old style serifs. Democrats have negative leading; Republicans set solid. Republicans use desktop typesetting technology; Democrats are still studying the size and expansion of the desktop and appropriate regulatory legislation.

Government workers can now order pre-shredded paper to save time.

If you backslant the typeface Aachen, does that produce and Aachen Back? I have brought some of you down to my level.

I'm working on a typeface called Ollie, which can't be seen by members of Congress.

It has been leaked to the *Washington Post* that the Department of Defense is working on a super-secret stealth desktop publishing system. It destroys typographic standards while leaving the *National Enquirer* intact.

What do you call a page produced by desktop publishing that has been shredded? Mercy killing

My answering machine has taken a vow of silence.

Historians have discovered the lost Shakespeare sequels: Romeo & Juliet II, Richard III III, Henry the IV, Part II, II, and Hamlet Meets Rambo—That Darn Dane.

I am working on high fibre transmission of bran data.

Trust Me

Emergency…emergency," the frantic caller sputtered. I'm here all alone and the computer typesetter won't… Can't…"

The situation called for cool heads and steady nerves. The person was alone and in trouble.

"Calm down," I said. "I'll talk you through."

"Give me your point size."

"What?"

"The specs command. What's the number?"

"Oh…12."

"OK, check your line length. Is it over 20 picas?"

"Yes, it's…that's the column command, right?"

"You got it."

"22 picas."

"Ragged?"

"No…justified."

"Good…you'll get through now. Read the leading value."

"Nine."

"OK, there's the problem. You've got a leading value less than your point size. Change it to 12 or 13."

"It's now 12."

"All right. Hit the justify key and stand back."

"I'm afraid."

"Trust me. Hit the key."

"I'm afraid…"

"You can do it."

"OK…it's …it's…running. The job justified."

"Print it out kid…bring it in."

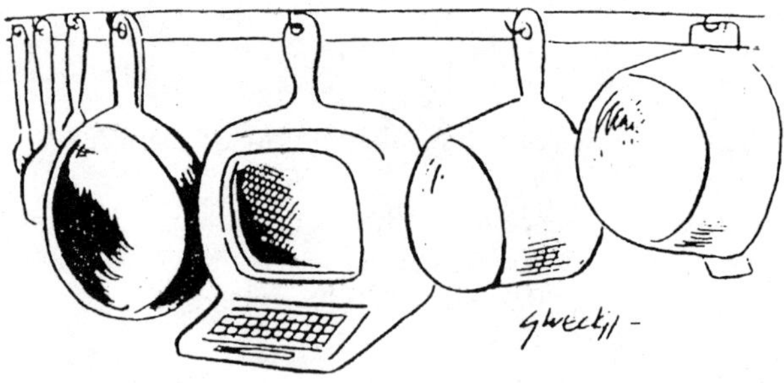

Some desktop publishing programs should be reported to OSHA.

Desktop publishing: never have so many used so little to do so so.

One of the major vendors wants to reach "unknowledgeable professionals" in order to sell them their brand of desktop publishing. Instead of using a Renaissance intellectual in their television promotions, they will probably use the three Stooges.

"Unknowledgeable professional"—like a surgeon that has not been to medical school. Or a politician that doesn't understand deficits.

There are four inviolable rules for typesetters:

1. Never get emotionally involved in a job. Revisions are just revisions.
2. Never say anything good about your machines or they will break immediately.
3. Never tell anyone how easy it is to set type.
4. View anyone who uses Souvenir as an unknowledgeable professional.

"The market could go in any direction," said security analysts quoted in *USA Today*. This is why these folks get the big bucks.

Chicago. The 1920s. A small group challenges the forces of darkness—"The unknowledgeables." Using desktop publishing they memo Al Capone to distraction. He fights back with guns, knives, and baseball bats. They retaliate with display type, footnotes and—egad!—bar charts. A showdown takes place at Union Station as the air is ablaze with paper and lead. Frank Nitti is felled by a well-kerned ligature. The mob is finished; it cannot fight. The Unknowlegeables. Watch for the sequel "Scarface Meets Souvenir" coming to your desktop soon.

This cannot be a very important industry. Geraldo Rivera has not done an investigative report on it.

At a desktop publishing show I saw the future. It was just as screwed up as the present.

Best overhead conversation of the conference:
"What do you use to produce pages?"
"A PC and a laser printer."
"How is it?"
"We all hate it intensely."
"Then why do you use it?"
"Because we own a magazine about desktop publishing."

To be fair, most of the people interested in desktop publishing were articulate and intelligent. This cannot be said for the people selling desktop publishing.

They don't really lie. They just have multiple revision levels of the truth.

Some of the revision levels of desktop publishing programs sound like star dates. One program is at version 3.11e.

The Ten Commandments are still at Rev. 1.0

One speaker said that anything that fits on a desk and sets type is desktop publishing. I said that a case of handset type and a small handpress would fit on a desk. The speaker said that it could not do graphics. OK, I said, how about a sheet of transfer type and a magic marker? Nope, they said, no multiple copies. All right, I countered, how about and IBM Composer, a drawing pen and a copying machine? No integration I was told. But not if operated by Siamese twins I finally replied,

3M is working on a new line of Post It leisure clothing called "Stick and Run."

One participant asked about all the bad design that desktop publishing would produce. Actually, there's adequate bad design with old technology. Perhaps we should have programs that monitor the page as it's being made up and then alert the operator to poor practices. Like ejecting a custard pie if they use Souvenir

Multitasking: the ability to do several things badly at the same time.

I half expected some of the presidential candidates to show up and announce that they were in favor of price supports for desktop publishing.

I love this industry. Where else can you meet someone you knew twenty years ago in hot metal who has a business card that says "desktop publishing consultant."

One program on exhibit went through two revision levels before it got to the show and one revision level during the show.

Revisions: from the Croatian "re-vise"—to squeeze again; to get more money for the next version.

Over half of the attendees at one session already had a photographic typesetting machine. Most of the rest already had laser printers. Some even used do matrix printers—they were the ones wearing open-toed sneakers.

A tobacco company has invented a smokeless cigarette; Japanese researchers have discovered odorless garlic; what we need now is a laser printer that won't set Souvenir.

Un-memory. For the storage of data you really do not care about. It is write only.

Pretty sad when crime is organized and crimefighting is not.

A plaintive question from a recent seminar on electronic publishing: "Do I have to put the entire page together electronically?" Paste-up dies hard.

Does the Pope use Altartop Publishing? Someone sent me a blurb about a tatooist who calls their work Fleshtop Publishing.

A new superhero—Captain Type—able to leap over ascenders with a single bound—boing!—faster than a line of leader dots—z-z-zip!—foe of the forces of good enough—bleech!—staunch defender of type, justification and the American way.

Computers can do more than people because they never have to stop and answer the phone.

At some seminars, the speakers cover electronic publishing from A to ZZZZZZ.

If they can train dolphins to find mines, why can't they be trained to do desktop publishing? We just need a waterproof mouse the size of a beach ball.

Richard Elliott Friedman's book "Who Wrote the Bible?" says that the Pentateuch was not written by Moses, as is commonly thought, but by a group of editors who did a cut-and-paste job in 450 B.C. Actually, it had to have been a chisel and mortar job or they had a Scroll Processor.

In an age of computers Moses would come down from the mountain with one dual-sided, quad-density floppy disk.

Q: How many desktop publishers does it take to change a lightbulb?
A: None. It's not a mouse function.

George Bush is not a wimp. He has already gone on the record that if elected he will pardon the designer of Souvenir.

One desktop publisher was caught mouse handed.

Typesetting machines and printers don't make enough of the right noises anymore. Used to be that we could tell what the machine was doing by the sounds it made. Remember lens turrets? Your knew there was a point size change when you heard clunka-daclunka-daclunk-ker-thump. Leader dots sounded like z-z-z-z-z-z-z–p but big leader dots were Z-Z-Z-Z-Z-Z-Z–P. Some users could tell what typeface was being set—serif faces seems to have an extra s-s-s-h at the end. Along came digital typesetters and all you heard was the er-r-r-r-p er-r-r-r-p of the leading motor. Laser printers are silent until they grab a piece of paper for imaging. Then you hear thm-m-m click-ah-rum-m-m-m thup. We should install artificial sound so that we can tell what the output device is doing…or not doing.

PCs have conditioned us to beeps. Just before the end of the world there will probably be a short beep and error message: Humanity has suffered an irrecoverable error and will shortly be erased. Check manual for details.

I received a call from a fellow traditionalist who had just gotten their InDesign software and exclaimed, "This not a desktop program; it's too good."

Photoshop is at revision 5, QuarkXPress is at 4.1 and PageMaker is at 6.5 —a revision gap?

Like me, many of you have suffered the frustration of computers that bomb out the worst possible time. At that point I want to strangle the darn machine and make it suffer. To vent this anger I've decided to start a company that will torture computers. Pages and pages of Jackie Collins and Harold Robbins text would be fed in plus the collected speeches of George W. Bush. Headlines from the *NY Post* would be scanned along with old police drawings of suspects. A video link to daytime television would be hooked up and speakers would blare country and western music for 24 hours. Lastly it would have to read this book. Computer Amnesty International may object to the latter punishment on artificial humanitarian grounds.

The Impersonal Computer. It ignores you.

The Desktop Publishing afternoon soap opera: "As the World Kerns"—in the last episode Portia caught Craig mousing around and threatened to trash his file folder. The Siamese twins, Jack and Jill, were in love with the same person, who had left for Borneo to become a desktop publishing consultant. Olivia discovered that she was the daughter of alien beings and would eventually metamorphose into a Souvenir letter R. Lance lost his fortune in the stock market by investing in bio-publishing futures—using microbes to set pages. Stay tuned for the next installment.

Overhead conversation:
"What did you do with your old equipment?"
"Sold it to Columbia."
"The university?"
"No, the country."

I still believe that there is typesetting graveyard where old machines go to die. There you will find the ATF B8 and the Fairchild 2000 piled on a Photon Zip beside a Fototronic. There's the Linofilm and the Quick and a rusting AM 707. All in a row are the 505 and 303 and a rare 404. See how the light reflects off the paper tape readers of the gray CG 2961 and the blue ACM 9000. Look, thousands of little markers made out of film and glass and plastic fonts: "Here lies Star Parts. RIP." The surge of emotion is too great; the memories are overwhelming.

New from Mattel: Desktop Barbie and Ken, complete with their own little PC and working laser printer (one dpi).

Some typefaces evoke a masculine feeling; some evoke a feminine feeling. Those in between are called transvestypes. There is terribly chauvinistic and all typefaces should therefore be unisex.

Archeologists have found what appears to be the operating manual for the Earth. One clue was the line, "This continent intentionally left blank" in Antartica.

Have you noticed how desktop publishing hype has slowed down and most programs are starting to emphasize features, now that they have some. They are repeating the same number games that traditional programs played for years: "I can kern 20 pairs automatically." "I can kern an infinite number." "I can kern one more than anyone else can, so there."

How to save money with corporate publishing. Don't go to any show, seminar, or conference that purports to tell you how to save money with corporate publishing.

Q: Will I go blind staring at a computer screen all day?
A: Only if you practice self abuse while editing.

Nautical publishing? Floating accents? Quad starboard? Stop me before I hurt myself.

Now that use of the term "desktop publishing " is trailing off, there is a period of anxious anticipation as we await the next round of hyperbole—sort of a buzz gap. We need a term that can fire our imaginations and stir our souls to new levels of confusion.

The Souvenir limitation Treaty is still begin negotiated in Geneva, Both sides would reduce their Souvenir arsenals simultaneously so that neither had a typographic advantage. However, a stumbling block has been the SDI—Souvenir Defense Initiative—the development of space-based printing and publishing.

Someone asked why I make fun of consultants. Besides politicians, who else is there to make fun of. Everyone else gets mad at me. I made one small jest a Benedictines and irate monks came after me. Fortunately, they had a vow of silence. If we could only get consultants to take such a vow.

The caller told the consultant that they had narrowed their decision down to an under $10,000 PC approach and over $300,000 system. "So?" the consultant asked. "Well, which way should we go?" "Take an average and get a $155,000 system."

I'm working on a publishing system that uses claymation. Little animated clay letters sing, "I heard it through the baseline..."

If Adidas can having clothing for sports, why not publishingware? Sweat bands for your fingers

Rumor of the week: Someone will introduce a laser printer with absolutely no resolution, for setting stealth manuals.

A printer that makes many copies is a copier, but a copier that makes only one copy is not a printer. A high-speed copier could also be a copier/duplicator. A printer that sets type is a typesetter, but a typesetter that sets typewriter print is not a printer. A high-speed printer is just a printer, although sometimes it is a printer/duplicator. There is no name for device that prints, typesets, copies and duplicates. Thank goodness.

With apologies to Oscar Wilde

Those who can, do.
Those can can't, teach.
Those who can't teach, teach others to teach.
Those who can't teach others to teach,
write books about teaching.
Those who can't write books about teaching, consult.

Consultants and politicians are almost the same. They promise things they can't deliver. They make great presentations. And they want to make the world safe for hypocrisy.

Some of the big consulting groups that have established their base in office automation are now promoting themselves as publishing experts. Ever downward.

Some typesetting folk fontificate.

One type firm is so rich it has a stretch imagesetter The layout people are called "page stylists."

Someone just dropped a note, "Why do you pick on consultants, when you're one of them?" Familiarity breeds contempt?

Remember the Contras? The real threat to Central America is a dissident group of guerrilla publishers called the Fontras. They have been known to attack villages and leave behind bizarre typographic symbols. They have received weapons from China capable of hundreds of lethal pages a minute. Congress is about to offer humanitarian aid: one year's worth of the Congressional Record. It has reached the point where petitions will be made to the united nations asking to ban the use of Souvenir for offensive purposes. Although it is rumored that Israel has a nuclear font capable of devastating the typography of an entire nation.

I don't have to do this you know. I gave up a promising career writing graffiti in train station men's rooms.

There is an interesting substitute for WYSIWYG—BYVE—Before Your Very eyes.

Having reached an age that requires bifocal eyeglasses, I have difficulty finding the right blend of distance and lens when working at a video screen. Moving my head back and forth and up and down causes passersby to think I'm doing a chcken impression.

Romano's Law: Data expands to fill the storage space available. I started with single-sided floppies and filled them to capacity. Then came double and quad density double-sided floppies and I filled them up. I jumped to a 10 megabyte rigid disk and filled it to the rim. Then I went to 20mb and and 40mb and 25omb filled then, too. I had a 500mb disk and filled it up as well. Now I have an 8 gigabyte hard disk and it's going fast. I need Weight Watchers for data...or Disk Addicts Anonymous. Stop me before I record on your disk!

Madonna's promotional material is set in Souvenir. Tacky for the trashy.

You are what you set. Some marketers, consultants, and show promoters use expanded outline fonts so they can say a lot about nothing

In the latest episode of "As The World Kerns." Lance has stolen the plans for stealth publishing but can't find them while Carlos is smuggling laser printers into the U.S. wrapped in cocaine (to get them through customs faster). Victoria admits to an affair with Gutenberg in another life and the U.S. Navy in this one. Rex decides on a sex change operation but can't decide which sex. And young Jimmy Bob runs away to become a consultant.

Souvenir is a font fatale.

"Souvenir: The Movie"—An amorphous blob from another planet with puce antennae and green skin invades earth and infiltrates the advertising world. Within a few years it advances to creative director and blends in.

Introducing ...the Desktop Desktop. Now you can actually use your desk as a desk—a novel concept. No computers and no printers to clutter the clutter. You don't have to publish, present, illustrate, or print on it. Just use it to lean on or stack the normal hodgepodge of a busy person. Call today. The first 20 callers get a free set of Ginsu knives.

The Corporate Cycle

1. Various departments within a large organization want to install publishing capability.
2. Management is confused so it does what it does best: it appoints a committee.
3. The committee is made up of competing departments and can't agree on an action.
4. A consultant is retained to act as referee.
5. Technology is finally recommended, the result of compromise analysis and personal prejudice.
6. It is too late to order for this fiscal year so it gets ordered for next fiscal year.
7. The technology is not in manufacture and support is limited. Productivity is off.
8. The poor performance is reported to management and it hires a different consultant.
9. The new consultant recommends that the company form a committee.

Archeologists have discovered that prehistoric man practiced stalagmite-top publishing. A Cro-Magnon newsletter was found incorporating graphics (pieces of several hairy Neanderthals).

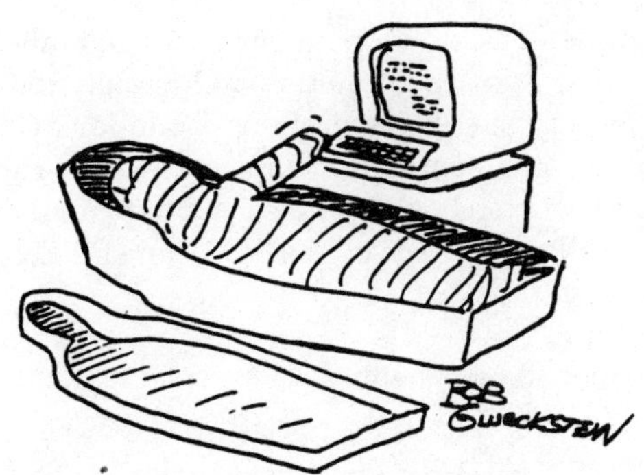

The great cataclysm comes and all mankind is destroyed save one man, one woman, and a desktop publishing operating manual. They decide to re-populate the race. Their first issue is a newsletter.

Everyone now has their own newsletter: Street people have one called "Ripple Review."

A priest, a rabbi, and a desktop publisher arrive in heaven. The gate keeper asks the priest "Did you lead a meaningful life?" The Priest says "I followed all the rules; I helped my flock; I supported the Pope; I led a good life." The same thing is asked of the rabbi, who replies: "I followed all the rules; I helped my congregation; I supported Israel; I led a good life." "Well," said the gatekeeper to the desktop publisher, "tell us about your life." "I have this newsletter that summarizes my life. It's four pages and set in Souvenir…"

Went to visit the New York Transit Authority. They have a laser printer covered with graffiti.

Why is it that most editors do their best work when they see galleys?

There is not truth to the rumor that a statue will be erected of me with a fig leaf over my mouth.

Q: What book will help one to understand the meaning and application of electronic publishing?
A: The Bible.

One of those slick desktop publications recently tried to describe what I do. They could not. Originally the reporter asked "You teach, edit publications, write for many more, author books, give seminars, organize meetings, run shows, serve on association boards, and consult for end users. How do you do all this?" "So-so," I said. " I'm still keeping my day job just in case."

Desktop publishing is neither.

Real men don't set Souvenir.

Please do not attempt to write drivel like this at home. I am a trained professional. Repeat, do not try this at home, it could be dangerous.

Those Washington "Kiss and Tell" books are nothing compared to my forthcoming expose of the typesetting industry—sort of "Kiss and Kern."

A patent has been issued on a genetically-engineered mouse. Honest. It is plug-compatible with the Macintosh and runs around the desktop putting pages together for you. The next step is an artificially intelligent genetically-engineered mouse that makes the same mistakes a human would. But first it would have to register as a Democrat.

Just returned from one of those super-colossal computer shows that give Roman orgies a bad name. Fortunately there were no vomitoria although some booths came close.

Matter, anti matter. If there is data, is there not also anti-data—a force in the universe which is the antithesis if information, like the Congressional Record or Internet e-business research reports?

The concept of the data navigator is that someday you will be able to travel through information as easily as a pilot travels through space. I, of course, see it another way: "Tailgunner to pilot, tailgunner to pilot, over." "Pilot here, over." "Alien information zeroing in at 12 o'clock high." "How many...how much..." "Looks like several megabytes, and it's...it's formatted." "Battle stations everyone. Activate all systems. Prepare the ultimate weapon." "The ultimate weapon!?" "Anti-data sector-to-sector missiles." "But you could wipe out information this planet. People will spend a millennia reading Jackie Collins and Harold Robbins. What's in those missiles?" "The works of Frank Romano..."

Typology. Governing your life by the faces of the type. As in "I feel Zapf Dingbatty today."

Desktop publishing is the hobgoblin of little minds.

We need a moratorium on new publishing products in order to gain experience in the misuse of what we already have. Sort of a publishing non-proliferation treaty

Unemployment would be about 2% higher if many of the people in between jobs didn't call themselves consultants.

A consultant speaks in generalities so that you can interpret their remarks and solve your own problems. In this respect, politicians, psychiatrists, and consultants are alike. However, politicians have a military.

Ever noticed how many programs many of us acquire as we seek the holy Grail of software? I have about ten word processing programs that I've gone through. At a recent seminar one of the speakers said that by 2000 there would be 21 million graphics programs. "That's not impressive," I said, "When you consider that it only represents about fifty users." They were not amused.

Is infinity squared more than infinity? Can something that is nothing be less? Can something that is everything be more? Can desktop publishing be more or less?

My doctor removed a splinter from my finger in his office. Is this desktop surgery?

More and more publishing programs are running on more and more platforms. Many routinely operate on both the Macintosh and Windows family. Interleaf runs on them as well as Apollo, DEC and Sun. In fact Interleaf may release a version that runs on a '58 Chevy.

My desk has become a desktop Bermuda Triangle. Stuff just disappears. Visionaries predict that someday all that paper will be in the computer…so I can lose it electronically.

Actually my desk is a Bermuda Rectangle.

It is a dimension of serif and sans, of time and type, between light and drop shadow. You are on a voyage into the graffiti of the human mind. You have entered the Souvenir Zone.

When the Government wants to set super secret material they don't load the fonts in their output device. They then stamp the empty page SECRET. Several clerks verify that the sheet is actually blank before filing it.

The Treaty of Versailles which ended WWI hostilities was hand calligraphed. The *Instrument of Surrender* in WWII was typed on a Varityper typewriter with proportional typographic fonts. The Korean War peace agreement was produced with hot metal typesetting. Agreements prepared after any future war will be chipped or painted on cave walls in Souvenir.

The stealth neutron bomb. This weapon destroys people who are not there, like those folks who vote in Chicago elections.

White-Out, the ultimate office tool. That little brush has really seen action. Some typists even use a roller. Me, I'm waiting for electronic White-Out. For people.

When you combine hyperpublishing with artificial intelligence you get one of those super-market tabloids.

In the latest episode of "As The World Kerns," Lance realizes that he has liberal tendencies and seeks to have them surgically removed. May Beth Ellen discovers the meaning of life and them misplaces it. Renphew goes from atheist to agnostic to unaffiliated deist during a stimulating brunch conversation. The Alpha twins fall in love with the Beta triplets which creates a fractional relationship.

Domino's Pizza Fax—pizza via your FAX machines. They're still having trouble with the pepperoni.

Souvenir: stealth typography.

Another person said that I'm not vicious enough. So I read the *New York Post* every day, scanned the *National Enquirer*, read Norman Mailer, listened to the collected works of Don Rickles and Don Imus, plus practiced in front of a mirror everyday. No one notices any difference.

Be sure to see the new film "Who Framed Harry Helvetica." It tells the tale of small type characters called Fontoons who live in typographic squalor in a place called Fontopolis. The evil Senator Souvenir, symbol of badness, attempts to condoize Fontopolis but meets resistance from Harry and the other fontoons who find the secret of algorithmic size and width modification in order to anamorphically condense the dastardly Senator to nothingness. The film ends on a happy note as Fontopolis is approved for urban renewal and all residents up their resolution.

I offended one consultant too many—woke up with a dead laser printer in my bed, my body covered with toner.

Three rules for editors

1. Never hyphenate a one syllable word.
2. Never change copy when it's in the bindery.
3. And never, never let them see you stet.

Pre-press: printing foreplay.

Is a mini maxi bigger or smaller than a maxi mini? The same goes for mini and micro mini. Is a mini mini a micro? And what is a maxi maxi, a grossi? Will computers someday come in Large Economy and Giant sizes? Or how about the ultimate size: Galactic.

Type...the final frontier. These are the voyages of the starship Souvenir, it's five-year mission to seek out alien typographic forms, to explore new serifs, and to boldly to go where no font has gone before—back to the Futura.

Through bio-engineering we have created a gerbil that can read and perform typesetting input by jumping up and down on the keys of keyboard. The only problem is the gerbil droppings in between the keys.

Gerbils work cheaper than mouses. This has created their own union to promote decent wages and good jobs. The industry is bracing for a mouse strike by training operators to go back to cursor keys. The mouse union organizer said "We are tired of being pushed around..."

Be sure to miss the new film "The Last Temptation of a Desktop Publisher."

Some desktop publishing pages are so badly done that they look like an explosion in an alphabet soup plant.

First there was the U.S. Mail. Then there was the Pony Express. Then special delivery got us mail delivery faster. Then the telegraph dits and dahs which Morse wrought. And the teletype which printed the messages out. Then bus same-day pouches got the material through. Then airline same-day pouch service to the airport. Then came Federal Express and next day delivery right to you. We have FAX and e-mail that get us messages almost instantly. What comes next?—e-mail that goes back in time so that messages are received before we need them.

Archaelogists have discovered that Stonehenge is actually a pre-historic publishing system. When viewed from two miles above it resembles a Souvenir lowercase o.

Optometrists report that video display operators should exercise their eyes on a regular basis. Jane Fonda is releasing her new Visual Workout Video—"Move those eyeballs; lift those lids."

Of mouses I have some advice
About the plural version 'mice'
Since the singular of dice is 'die'
Shouldn't the singular of mice be 'mi'?
And to those who may suffer
Some degree of dismay
The plural of mouse is 'mouses' I say

Cajun publishing: blackened pages.

We asked one thousand doctors—if stranded on a desert island, which would they prefer: Pagemaker, InDesign, Ventura, or QuarkXPress? Two out of three still preferred Bayer aspirin.

Souvenir: Smurf typography.

In a recent survey Harvard University students stated that most classes put them to sleep. This is to prepare them for future business meetings.

More and more of you tell me how upset you are with suppliers that outdate their equipment at a very rapid pace. Go and try to get a 5-year old computer repaired and see what happens. We're not even talking five years since some machines came out. The check often does not clear before a new machine hits the market. We should pay them in dollars that obsolete as quickly as their technology.

Spelling checkers watch your words
For alphabets gone awry
Missing the metamorphosis of curds to turds
So trust, but verify

An idealist doesn't use a spelling checker; a realist usually does. A cynic also uses one, but doublechecks with a dictionary.

I activated the spelling and grammar checkers, the antonym and synonym finders, the cliché and sexist changers, the style and pomposity evaluators and the machine suddenly came to life. The screen glowed for a while and the message came up "I think; therefore I am. " It should have been original, at least.

Neurotics design pages in thin air. Psychotics print them on transparent paper.

Bumper sticker of the week: Desktop publishing happens.

Nightmare on Em Street: widows and orphans are attacked by double daggars wielded by bold hobos.

All the competitors in the computer industry are going to continue to pool their introductions of equipment and systems. In fact they may all introduce the same machine.

If you scan color separations fast enough, you can send them back in time, thus delivering them yesterday.

Hot metal: topless typesetting.

How many desktop publishers does it take to change a light bulb? Only one, so long as there is an 800-number to call for assistance.

What we really need is a utility program that converts glitzy graphs and charts back into tables of alphanumeric data. Graphs are great, but data is greater.

Have you been to one of those seminars like "Dare to Love" or "Dare to Hate?" I'm starting one called "Dare to Kern" or even "Dare to Float An Accent."

The challenge of today's technology is not to make people computer literate but to make computers people literate. And that's not artificial intelligence; that's real intelligence.

The American Civil Liberties Union has said that it must often aid real sleaze bag types of people to protect the civil rights of all. Therefore they have decided to defend anyone who uses Souvenir.

What do I do for a living? I mouse around.

Oxymoron: an electronic mechanical.

A consultant is compensated heckler

Computer literacy means you are knowledgeable about computers; visual literacy means you are knowledgeable about design and layout. Literacy literacy means you know what you're talking about.

Technical jargon recently overhead: the gzinta is connected to the gzouta. Gwhata?

Can you have a system with real time and artificial intelligence? Isn't that what digital clocks are for?

A book about IBM could be called "The Soul of a Blue Machine."

The computer said "Read my bits..."

What do you do with a 30 line halftone screen, the usual result of most 300 dpi printers? You make it the size of Rhode Island so that astronauts can see a picture.

"All of our computers are down." Try telling them a funny computer story to cheer them up. Sort of artificial humor, like this book.

Robo Publisher: bionic finger for blazing input; mouse control by eyeball movement (blinking is clicking); on-line access to the recorded works of mankind—coming soon to a desktop near you.

The computer had a conniption
The virus was a warning
So what is the prescription?
Input two aspirin and fax me in the morning.

Computer spelling checkers are part of a plot to destroy our ability to spell. Throughout history (and even before that) good spellers have always displaced bad spellers. Look at the Phoenicians. They could spell and thus ruled the Mediterranean. The fact that they were the first to have an alphabet so no one know if they were right or wrong is besides the fact. The Renaissance was brought about because of spelling; only good spellers could spell it. If you want to rule the world, be a good speller.

It is now official: Souvenir will be cryogenically frozen and placed in a time capsule for a future when a cure may be found.

I activated my spelling checker and then listened closely. The computer mumbled "I before E, except after C..." I'll bet it even counts on its fingers and toes when no one is looking.

If a rhetorical question has no answer, does a rhetorical answer have no question? Like the replies politicians provide.

The president is naming a Design Czar to cabinet rank, who will prepare a national strategy to combat bad design. A campaign is being developed with the theme "Souvenir—Just Say No!"

Hypertext is being hyped as information with all four dimensions. This means that a terminal can actually access data that is back or forward in time. You can read memos that you will write tomorrow today and change what you predicted yesterday to match the results of tomorrow. This is the perfect tool for the corporate office since we can get work done yesterday by people who were out then but will start today because they're off tomorrow.

So I packed my portable TV/video player, portable computer, portable cellular telephone, portable FAX, and portable printer. I had six bearers who carried by portable products on their heads as my safari wended its way through the office. The next step is to make people portable.

There are two rules of consulting:
1. Never take a job you cannot handle
2. Never turn down a job.

Microprocessor: a very small Cuisinart.

My typesetting machine is so old, when I need replacement parts I have to wait for a donor.

If the U.S. Constitution had been produced using a word processor it would still be in revision. There's lot to be said about writing things out. You think twice before changing anything. Actually, you think twice before writing anything.

The Stealth Bomber costs $2.4 billion each. Batteries not included.

Some computer programs should be arrested for cruel and unusual icons.

Desktop publishing association: a gang that couldn't set straight.

In the latest installment of "As The World Kerns"—Rex goes font hunting and bags a Bodoni; Mary Lou leaves home without her American Express card and is severely beaten by Karl Malden; Jason has an affair with his personal computer but it leaves him for an electronic toll booth attendant and the Capricorn twins forget which is which and then decide that it doesn't matter.

In a new book on the future of robots and human intelligence, the author contends that within the next 50 years, robots will pass the threshold of humanlike abilities. With miniaturization down to the atomic level, future robots will transcend the term "intelligence" as we now understand it. They will become our companions, workmates and heirs. I think this may happen. Therefore decided to leave all my worldly possessions to my microwave who will then take care of the blender and toaster. However, I have disinherited the TV set and lawn mower, for reasons most people would understand.

Video tape players allow us to rent movies that we would have never paid money to view in a theater but are okay to watch on television, where mediocrity is the sight to see. Reality, you see, is only 525 lines.

My kids are growing up with heavy metal; I grew up with hot metal.

There are now seven desktop publishing associations. Each has about ten members. They all intend to band together under the leadership of Col. Qaddaffi.

Tired of perfection? Run your copy through a miss-spelling checker to create random errors. It will make you appear to be more human.

They want to store nuclear waste in outer space. Let's put the people who create nuclear waste in outer space.

ICBM—really heavy metal.

Transcendental typesetting—alignment on an astral plane.

Some typographic associations are so reactionary, staff members wear pointed white hoods and burn the letter Q on front lawns.

The technology is almost ready for each of us to publish personal newsletters of our lives. You would issue a daily publication covering your previous 24 hours, with text, graphics and, of course, photographs. When someone asks you how you are, you just give them the last few issues to read. What's new? Easy, slip them the latest installment. What did you do on vacation? Hand them a bound volume. You can interview yourself or even have your own centerfold. Andy Warhol said that each of us would be famous for 15 minutes. Now you can leave a complete record of your life. How many minutes is that?

People who deal in rumors have no dpi.

I mean it's really getting out of hand. The computer press is now reporting on the Intel 586 microprocessor chip when we haven't fully exploited the 486 version. Motorola has the 68060 and folks are yakking about the 68050. George Washington Carver created 101 products from the peanut. He said, "It's what you do with what you have that counts." We need to apply technology better, not wait for better, technology to apply.

My computer and I both got a virus at the same time. Blue Cross does not cover PCs, however, Medicare will if the PC is over 75 years old and lives in Miami.

Did you know that the first item printed by Gutenberg was not the Bible. It was an indulgence, which left certain areas blank to be filled in with the name of the recipient and the amount paid. The first product of the technology called printing was a form! One of the first items produced by desktop publishing back in 1984 was an IRS Form 1040. Nothing changes. We just transferred payment from God to Caesar.

One senator wants to make unwanted fax sending a punishable offense. He then sent faxes on the subject to a number of other parties.

Maybe 300 dpi is all we deserve.

You're showing your age if you remember when a copier was a sheet of carbon paper, a workstation was a blotter, and fax transmission was the kid who delivered the mail. I even remember when elevators had automatic voice recognition: you said "5th floor please" to the operator and they sped you right there.

I figured it out. You create a child. Virtually no charge. Sixteen years later the kid costs a fortune, an eating machine that wears a Walkman. Just like some systems—a publishing pit with a mouse.

An Ode To Image Processing

Dot or spot, what have we begot?
Little things mean a lot
Pixel and pel, numbers in a cell
Isn't techno jargon swell?
Spots are hard to classify
The building blocks of "spi"
Printer resolution, low or high
Pels are spots by another name, all the same
Just a ball of fame
Pixels add in levels of gray,
Lots of bits to convey
So scanner, screen images you may portray
Dots are spots that are not alone,
Giving photos half a tone
An optical illusion, let it be known
Put them in a pot and what've you got
RIPs and bit maps and all of that lot

Desperately Seeking Sanity—the story of the typographic industry as it phases through technology and terminology and just plain Oh Gee.

Now that we have pre-designed style sheets for people who cannot design, why not pre-written texts for people who cannot write? We will all look and sound alike.

If the universe is actually a computer, where does it call for service? Does IBM make calls to infinity? At what hourly rate? Imagine, an eternity without an upgrade, except for an occasional black hole.

As I get older, My RAM is turning to ROM. Every time I remember something new, it replaces something old. I need tape backup

Computer—The Adjective. Why are we so intent on describing things as computer-this or computer-that? The computer part is often understood. The term "computer typesetting" was necessary when all other typesetting was non computer, but now that all typesetting is computer typesetting, the adjective is redundant. Like computer publishing or computer pre-press. Now I could understand computer dentistry or computer gynecology until these areas also go the way of all electronics. Tune in next week for Electronically—The Adverb.

Scientists have finally discovered the secret of DNA: PostScript. This PDL (Pre-natal Description language) carries outline data for the type of person you will become. Sizing is of course dynamic with fill routines based on color. However, Adobe still will not reveal what the hints on each chromosome do for people of low resolution.

When production rates get too high or do not meet expectations, what does industry do? It automates. Therefore, let's automate Congress. We can program computers to be liberal or conservative, or even middle of the aisle, to give long, unnecessary and meaningless speeches, and to accept input from computer lobbyists. But don't use an intelligence checker on Congressional software; you might break it.

There, son, up in the night sky. See those stars as the ancients saw them. See Orion, The Hunter, and there, the computer constellation RAM, The Memory. Those stars all in a row are LAN, The Network, and there on the horizon Giga, The Byte.

Some folk suffer from mental graffiti.

If you have tiny hands, you need a mini mouse.

Apollo has announced a new workstation for 3D graphics. Actually, I would like to see a 4D machine...one that not only looks behind an object but also looks into it soul. Sort of a metaphysical mode.

Souvenir Dingbats—redundant redundancy.

Does this make sense? We use off-the shelf, inexpensive software running on off-the shelf, inexpensive, desktop computers and then spend thousands of dollars to upgrade them with memory and peripherals to get them where we want them and then train people how to use them. We need off-the-shelf operators, but then we would need bigger shelves.

Computers use logic circuits; some people do not.

The NRA says that computers are more dangerous than guns and should be registered. Only the other day I tried to hold up a gas station with my Macintosh.

My IBM ThinkPad portable personal computer battery had run down and I had to have it jump started. A kindly truck drive cabled it to his 18 wheeler and revved the engine. Its data is now somewhere on Mars.

Why aren't there any hyphenation programs for Latin?

Why is abbreviate such a long word?

It's now official. The *New York Times* say that we are not far away from creating artificial life. They said that computer viruses are just another extension of humanity into an electronic world. That ultimately machines will be people and people will be machines. Instead of saying "I'm wearing a digital watch," the watch will say "I'm wearing a digital person."

We are now so enamored of typography on our video screens that someday they may have to sell an anti graphic adapter board for those who want monospaced characters.

Now that Intel has a 64-bit microprocessor, Motorola has decided to leapfrog the competition and go directly to a 128-bit chip. When running at full speed, the machine will heat Minnesota.

My answering machine never has any answers.

They have discovered that there is a parallel universe where everything is the opposite of this universe. For instance, there is my opposite: thin, handsome, a good speller. Unfortunately he's trapped in a world where those are negative attributes.

If there is matter and anti-matter, this also means that if there is type, there must be anti-type, negative resolution that sucks dots into oblivion, Like kids eating M&Ms.

The Ayatollah says that anyone who uses Souvenir is an insult and should be eliminated.

I bought one of those really cheap monitors. The cursor says in one place and you have to move the screen around.

Floppy disks are no longer floppy as they become smaller and smaller. They went from 8" to 5-1/4" to 3-1/2" and now they may become 2-1/2". Floppies have thus migrated from the maxi to the mini to the micro to the, what else, dinky disk.

Let us now praise people who think rather than machines that think.

The personal computer industry is taking a page from Detroit's book—planned obsolescence. Since the dawn of the microprocessor chip we have seen innumerable models and revisions of models. The Apple II of today is a different creature than it was when it was introduced. The same is true of PC models. Today's Macintosh is nothing like the original Macintosh from 1984. We are accelerating change at such a pace that there will be annual model changes and computers will be designated to their model and year: I have a vintage "'82 XT that is in mint condition," or "my '85 Mac-Plus was only used on weekends by a little old hacker from Cupertino," or even "My '87 PS-50 is being recalled…"

At a recent trade show, a software company did not have their product ready, so they displayed a picture of the package. I tried to buy it with a picture of a check.

The age of miniaturization is upon us. All machines are shrinking. Computers are getting so small that they may someday be implanted in people. It might not be unusual to go to a maintenance depot and see a batch of people sitting around on shelves with tags hanging from their ears as they wait to be serviced.

One scientist says that someday humans may marry robots. Just what we need—robo kids.

The age of "mind link" will be upon us, futurists predict. This means that we may have mind-to-mind fax. You're sitting in a meeting and paper starts to exit from your breast pocket.

Are you a victim of the real M&Ms: meetings and memos.

Mind Links will require a new form of message dialing. You will have to think of another mind's number. There will still by busy signals and wrong mind numbers. If there is no answer, the party is dead. For privacy you can get an unlisted mind but those computer calls will still get through. You, yourself, will become your own mobile phone.

I just trademarked the copyright symbol ©™...or did I copyright the trademark symbol TM©. In any case, if you use either one, send me money.

If you are into hyper text you can hyper write and then use your spelling checker before you actually create the copy.

Hyper text may allow you to send copy back in time so you can dangle your participle yesterday.

Microwave ovens give us hyper food: Fax gives us hyper messages; the SST gives us hyper flight; and TV programs give us hyper heartache.

So what if the Pentagon paid $269 for a washer. This was no ordinary washer—it was a stealth washer. The hole was around the outside with the solid part in the middle.

Reincarnation: not so instant replay.

There must be computer reincarnation. My Macintosh occasionally lapses into IBM 1401 code.

The U.S. Navy is training dolphins for "guard" duty at submarine bases. I have it on good authority the Naval scientists are working on a stealth dolphin.

Typography: text appeal.

When I pass on I would like to be scanned at high resolution instead of cremated. Then I can be reincarnated as a piece of clip art and thus haunt desktop programs from inside the software. Instead of a virus you will have a poltergeist. You will need a computer ghost buster or an electronic exorcist.

Just as I wrote that last paragraph my monitor spun around 360 degrees and the screen went black. Can't anyone—or anything—take a joke anymore?

If there was a typographical error in the Constitution, would the framers say "The quill did it?"

Rumor: no sooner said than said.

Ronald McIntosh tells me that there are indeed hyphenation programs for Latin (his) and that (guess who?) the Vatican has one of them. This, of course, is known as holy hyphenation and is not discretionary. The Pope may hyphenate ex cathedra by logic, dictionary or revelation.

Saw an ad in one of those publishing publications for a desktop folding unit. You insert your floppy disk, then…

Desktop publishing color is a gray area.

There is nothing wrong with Souvenir that a complete redesign would not cure.

The *Times* called a new science Virtual Reality. Virtual memory means that there is no real limit on memory storage and access. Virtual Reality says that there is no real limit on what you can experience. You could travel to Uranus without ever leaving earth, although one subject supposedly says he already had that experience by smoking a Snickers bar in the Men's Room of the Plaza hotel.

Desktop publishing is artificial publishing. It's not real.

Desktop 16-bit color, 32-bit color—the result in most cases is just 2-bit color.

Computer consultant—one who reads the manual.

The cycle of product development: specification, pre-prototype, prototype, alpha and beta versions, released version, corrected version, upgrade, modified upgrade, revisions 2 and 4, complete re-development, fixes, upgrades, revisions...

"Clone" can be good or bad depending on your point of view. When comparing your product to competitors, clone can mean that yours is an exact copy of theirs (good); or, that theirs is a ripoff copy of yours (bad).

Irony. Federal Express just delivered my new fax machine.

Voice input is going to wipe out mouses. This has created a problem in the computerized rodent world. The mice have their own union (United Mouse Workers) to promote new jobs for mice and protect agaist cheap foreign mouse labor. The industry has been bracing for a mouse strike by training operators to go back to cursor keys. The mouse union organizer said "We are tired of being pushed around."

Michael and Gabriel, the archangels, are concerned about an impending re-organization in Heaven. The cherubim and seraphim have not taken sides, Gabriel has been tooting his on horn a little bit too much lately.

Jim Mattingly writes to tell of "neuro script" which is an Idea Description language (IDL) that allows thoughts to be translated into realities. This can be quite dangerous if you tend to daydream. Fortunately the first version will be at very low resolution (5 dpi), restricting you to half thoughts and lousy ideas. Bright ideas will require one million dpi

Wang Labs is using a special electronic stylus for their new system. They feel that the pen is mightier than the mouse.

Un-memory. For the storage of data that you really do not care about. It's write-only so you can store it away, but you can't read it. The military is going to use it for super secret documents.

This year we have seen a plethora of Macintosh shows, Mac New York, Mac Washington. How about Mac Mars? Call when you get back.

A lost manuscript of Dante's was found recently. In an early draft of the Divine Comedy, those dammed to the inferno were 300 dpi and those blessed to enter Paradisio were 1000 dpi or more.

The Oxford English Dictionary now defines "desktop publishing" in one of its 20 volumes. Fortunately, no one knows which one.

Recent patent rejections: a combination electric shaver and mouse, a combination mouse and vibrator, and a mouse that moves in three dimensions for people who practice zen publishing.

Souvenir: punk type.

Don't you just love those makeover articles where one designer second guesses another designer by re-doing the first designer's work? Let's not stop with desktop publishing. Let's wipe the smile off the Mona Lisa and get Whistler's mother off that rocking chair.

Hip mother: "You should e-mail more often…"

Desktop publishing pages are actually better than they look.

Kerning—what a concept.

As computers take over more and more of the work of human beings, what will be left for us to do? Throw the switch. To off.

The un-publishing program takes completely assembled pages and reduces them to their basic elements: text and graphics. It's a version of Desktop Chaos.

United Nations has declared the earth a Souvenir free zone.

Semiconductor manufacturers, in a feat of sub-microscopic legerdemain, have reduced the state of New Jersey to a computer chip. Motorola says it will counter with Texas and Intel has already started to work on Alaska.

Computers are now being used to teach sex education according to *U.S. News & World Report*. The interactive Windows-based programs teach teenagers about the birds and the bees with RAMs and ROMs. One kid was somewhat confused, trying to put a condom on a mouse.

There should be a Constitutional amendment on Souvenir burning. In favor, of course.

Pets can now be implanted with an electronic "dog tag" that emits identification information. You can also get an electronic flea collar. I'm working on gerbil fax.

They are going to cut back on the stealth bomber program The planes will now be fuzzy instead of invisible.

Mathematicians have calculated Pi to 480 million decimal places. And I still can't find a pica ruler that's accurate.

Apple is spending a fortune trying to create excitement about a new buzz term: desktop media. The singular is desktop medium, which is a fortune teller with a crystal fax machine for immediate reports from the hereafter.

I packed my portable computer, portable FAX, portable copier and portable calculator along with a portable wagon to carry it all. I can see the day when an 18-wheeler is stopped on some highway and the state trooper asks what you're hauling—"Just my portable possessions, " you reply.

Drug abuse. Alcohol abuse. And, of course computer abuse. Go out and abuse a computer today.

And should we not complain about how computers have abused people?

In Hawking's "Brief History of Time" we learn that scientists had developed mathematical models for black holes (or stealth stars) long before there was physical evidence of their existence. Economists have also found a black hole—it's called the Federal Budget.

Power of the press belongs to those
who own the press.
Real power of the press belongs to those
who know how to use the press.
The profit in the power of the press belongs to those
who sell paper and ink.

Desktop publishers dream in 300 dpi.

This book was instructive. I learned that you really do not want to go back in time. First of all it would mean having to deal with Revision level 1.0 of every desktop publishing, computer publishing, and word processiing program I could not bear to do that again.

A light year is the distance traveled by light in one year. I think we need a different unit of measurement for typesetting—the light pica—the time it takes light to travel 6 points. Then when someone asks how long it will take to do a job, you can respond "About 20 light picas." Of course, the bold pica is something else entirely.

In the *New York Times* computer column, the author stated that you should never buy software at Revision level 1.0. That means that all suppliers will have to start at level 2.0 when they introduce new software. NeXT start at .1 and is now at .8 on its way to 1.0 thinking that when reached 1.0 they would have stable program. Now they will have to rethink that strategy. Of course, if one purchased 1.0 of new software, suppliers would never sell anything and could not afford to advertise in newspapers that tell readers not to buy something that is new. Maybe we should start at level 10.0 and them work backward so the 1.0 becomes the ultimate version. The article was probably a first draft, level 1.0 if you will, that got into print by accident.

Scientists now say that the basic building block of the universe is the quark. There is debate. I say it's a one point em leader dot.

US Air is now making as many flights as the stealth bomber.

The stealth bomber evades enemy radar. Wouldn't it have been cheaper if it had one of those highway radar detectors used to avoid state troopers on the dashboard? Right next to the statue of Casper Weinberger. The pilot hears the detector and then slows down.

I think my cats are leading a secret life. The answering machine has meow messages on it and one of them now has a tiny beeper.

Congress has decided to put nuclear missiles on trucks and the stealth bombers on hold.

We could send Souvenir to Mars but there are international treaties on pollution in outer space. We can only pollute the earth. So far our planet is the only toxic waste dump in the solar system.

To make up for losses in the automobile business, General Motors, Ford, and Chrysler will soon convert their production lines to the manufacture of Star Wars' collectibles. They will have annual models, flashy advertising, and eventual competition from the Japanese.

A Ford laser printer? Output measured in picas per gallon.

What You See Is What You Get
The phrase should make us all upset
And for those acronyminal
WYSIWYG's criminal
In abuse of the alphabet

I called the computer to check on an error in my bill. It said the person did it.

The stealth bomber may be out of sight to radar but its price is out of sight to Congress.

The Federal Budget may be produced with desktop publishing. The 1999 budget will be completed in the year 2002.

Photographic halftones are produced by placing a screen between the original image and the photo-sensitive material. The light is then "filtered" through the screen. So…

I think that I shall never see
A picture screen at 133
When groups of spots are all arrayed
And pseudo grays are thence displayed
Electronic pixels are made by fools like me
But only God can make them
photographically

What do you give someone who uses a spelling checker? A proofreader.

There's a mouse replacement that controls computers via human body language—twitches, brain waves, body temperature. During testing a subject sneezed and bombed spreadsheets across three states.

The Voyager space probe has sent back digital images of Neptune. A Gramm-Rudman low-budget version of the unmanned craft will send post cards from Pluto.

I've got gigabytes of memory
And gigahertz of speed
But no matter how much I have
There's always more I need

I've got megabytes of RAM
And mega-mips galore
But even with all that
I'm still in need of more

My hardware costs keep climbing
My software cost—oh my
I guess I'll still be buying
Until the day I die

And when I reach the Pearly Gates
It will just be like before
An infinity of upgrades
An eternity of more

I have a PC that utilizes cold fusion energy. It rubs two programmers together in a jar.

Souvenir Outline: a gutless typeface.

The salesman said the the PC would cut my work in half. I bought two.

Many of us still do not know the difference between a dial tone and a halftone.

Dear Ruth Westheimer:
I am in a quandary. I like the Mac operating system but it's proprietary and closed, where Windows is more prevalent. But it is being replaced by NT which is almost as graphical as the Mac but not as multitasking as UNIX. UNIX also is struggling with competing screen representations. What should I do?
Signed: Confused.

Dear Confused:
Establish a meaningful relationship with your workstation. The perfect operating system may never come along so find one that you can relate to. Perhaps you should live together for a while. And always practice safe publishing.

The ultimate excuse: the computer is in the mail.

IBM enlightened the audience by declaring that in publishing workstations they may do something or everything or not, sooner or later or not, with Microsoft or Adobe and others, or others, with OS/2 or UNIX or something else, or everything else, or nothing else, or not, maybe.

A Xerox speaker told of future information highways. I could only wonder if there would be information State Troopers. Will data packets have teeny-tiny radar detectors?

He spoke of the two-way electronic book, where the reader reads the book and the book reads the reader. Be sure to dress before opening the book.

Congress now supports desktop publishing. Appropriate.

We came up with a buzzterm for un-computer, non-electronic, all-natural technology. It's called "human."

Desktop publishing is like self service gasoline, or in the case of Exxon, self spilling gasoline.

A bumper sticker said "That day of judgement is at hand." The day of integration is also at hand. However, it may be the same day.

I only know what I read in the trade press, and it scares the Souvenir out of me.

What do you call what I do to Souvenir: character assassination.

New computer models do not really obsolete previous models so much as they cause pc envy.

One day all the computers went down, so we broke the emergency glass. Inside, the instruction said "Think for a change."

I don't care how fast computers ever go; their output still has to pass through the mailroom.

The end result of some desktop publishing should be called schlock doc.

Mechanization—Look ma, no muscles!
Automation—Look Ma, no hands!
Artificial Intelligence—Look ma, no brains!

Financial analysts have every hope and assurance that the market will be successful, but if it isn't they knew all the time that it wouldn't and warned us about it.

The phone company, a uniquely monopolistic institution, which, in failing to automate its technology, is attempting to automate its customers. Press 1 if you are pissed about pressing numbers instead of talking to a real person.

With computer viruses rampant, it is important for you to practice safe computer typesetting. If you kern too closely, use protection.

There are said to be 100 million electronic workstations in the American workforce, counting PCs, computer terminals, etc. However, there are only 50 million workers. What could be over 50 million terminals doing? They could be operated by the deceased people who are said to still collect Social Security. Or are they stealth workers created by the CIA?

What happens if you select a 20% tint of white?

You have heard the term vaporware. I say there is a better term for something that is only said to exist: Stealthware.

The Australians have developed a radar that can see the stealth bomber, thus negating billions of dollars in development. Congress is studying other ways to waste the funds earmarked for stealth technology. Like stealth medical care or stealth Social Security.

A recent letter said I should impart more wisdom and insight in this column so here goes: 1. Never buy a machine with a serial number under 100, 2. Never assume the service person has spare parts with them, and 3. Never buy anything from a salesman named Swifty.

The Apple/Microsoft font approach is the first stealth font technology. Think of it as an outline font technology. No, think of it as outline font without the outline.

Can you picture Microsoft creating a font library. Heck, they didn't know there was an earthquake until someone noticed that all the lowercase l's were obliqued.

Adobe took its first five years to produce 590 PostScript fonts. This means that Microsoft could take until 2001 to have 500. Sure, they'll have 500 fonts but all of them will be Souvenir.

At a meeting in 1986 on font standards, Microsoft asked for suggestions on a new name for their font approach. Someone yelled "Why not call it Off?

How to cut drug use in the U.S.—have cocaine distributed by desktop computing dealers.

Exxon is thinking of re-introducing their 1975 word processor. Programmers want to make sure words don't spill out and pollute the business office.

The Supreme Court has determined that life begins at Revision 1.0.

The stealth bomber finally left the ground. It had to; it is too expensive to be a stealth jeep.

He also said that just as people once leased their bodies, that in the year 2009 we will lease our brains—furnished or unfurnished?

He even added that if you want to be immortal, you should digitize yourself. We could even have italic people. We don't need them any bolder, but condensing them would free up space on busses.

One person I know does not have a brain to lease, but does have an ego big enough to condo-ize.

To digitize yourself you will need the new Scan-Man personal hand held scanner and electric shaver. It has 256 protoplasm levels and creates a complete bit map of your body. A special utility program increases your resolution.

What do you call a typographic egotist? A Donald Trump Mediaeval.

The symbol of technology
Is not computing or the TV
It's a little box held in the hand
Remote control at your command
To turn machines off or on
From the comfort of the chair you're on
The result is both a seat that's numb
And little crutches for your thumb

Just bought a Zen workstation. It comes with a multi-lifetime guarantee.

Scientists have reduced all matter in the universe to six particles: Quark, basic building block of the sub-atomic world (and its faster version, The Quark Express); the Proton, composed of three Quarks (unless it's four which is a full house); the Electron, which flows through electrical wires (the only charge that is charged for); the Neutrino, the eunuch of particles with no charge and no mass and thus billions of them pass through our bodies everyday (but take longer through my body); the Muon, a component of cosmic rays, which means there is definitely a Muon over Miami; the Tau, which no one understands; and the Z, which only existed in the orgasmic moments of the Big Bang and the creation of the universe as we know it. Typographers know that there are really only three basic particles: the Thin, En and Em and that the universe is only the result of a computer error brought about by bad hyphenation and justification.

In recent issue of one of those weekly business magazines there was one article telling how computers are getting smaller, more portable, and more powerful, and another article telling how computers were getting bigger and more powerful. No wonder people read the *National Enquirer*.

Kids can now fax their Christmas lists to Santa using a new troll free number.

Eventually our money will be valued by its resolution, as in "Do you have 20dpi bills for a Cdpi note?" Inflation will result in the loss of scan lines. Ft. Knox will store bitmaps.

Andy Warhol said the someday everyone will be famous for fifteen minutes. I say that someday everyone will have a type named after them. A billion fonts named Wong?

My New Year's resolution: 900dpi.

Three was lots of discussion about hypertext. I suggested electronic Valium.

I saw the NeXT workstation as it played Bach, had a game of chess with itself and searched the works of Shakespeare for a quote. In the real world, it would probably be playing Musak, during a game of tic-tac-toe while searching the works of Harold Robbins for intelligence.

If "good enough" describes things that are less than perfect, why not use "bad enough" to describe things that are less than imperfect. A 5.0 on the Richter Scale is bad, but a 1.0 is only bad enough. There is probably a point where good enough and bad enough overlap. It is called Souvenir.

If an original is good and a copy is good enough then a copy of a copy is bad enough and a copy of a copy of a copy is just plain bad.

So I asked Leona Helmsley what she thought about the changing world of electronic publishing and printing—"Only the little people use desktop publishing," she harumphed.

Another Christmas has passed with no toys to assemble. So I took the microwave apart. I discovered what makes it so hot in there—an h&j routine tries to hyphenate a three-letter word so the art director can have a light ragged right with no hypehenation and letterspacing.

The entire AT&T telephone network was messed upon day; the vital communications of business and industry were in jeopardy; and then someone says "Computers are not trustworthy."

Congress said the computer did it.

In a bold move to balance the Federal deficit Congress is considering a tax on typographical errors. The "typo tax" will raise billions of dollars and create a cabinet level position "Typo Czar."

They want to build a stealth hangar for the stealth airplane. This is known as stealth logic. Anyone will be able to find where they parked the plane—just look for the sign that says "Reserved for stealth bomber. All other planes parked here will be disappeared."

Virtual memory may have to do with computers, but at my age it's beginning to become virtual forgetfulness.

I remember when old-time graphic arts folk got together and got tipsy. Now a new generation gets together and get technical. Either way, I don't understand them. And I will not sing "Melancholy Baby."

Bell Labs has a new computer that works with light. Heck, my toaster works with both light and dark.

My PC must have a virus. It modemed in sick with the message "No DOS today."

It is now official. Adobe will introduce a PostScript RIP that is so fast, running at full speed would slow down the rotation of earth, sending Souvenir back in time.

1975
How many terminals on a CPU?
1985
How many CPUs on a network?
1995
How many CPUs in a terminal?
2005
How many CPUs on a chromosome?

Programs now run under almost all operating system. I know one that runs under CP/M, DOS, OS2, MAC OS, ULTRIX, AIX, AUX, UNIX, LINUX, and also on a 1987 Yugo.

You could have a PC the size of a credit card. Then it would be a PPC—Piddly Personal Computer.

A computer named Deep Thought lost a chess game to a second-level human chess champion. So far computers 0, humans 1. A binary score.

Maybe we should be putting more intelligence in people and less in computers. You can only have artificial intelligence if there is real intelligence to emulate.

There is only one way to protect your computer from those nasty viruses that are spreading. Put a condom on every floppy disk.

Kids are allowed to use calculators when they take some tests. But only one battery.

Whether you think you can or you think you can't—you're right.

It's what you learn after you know it all that counts.

What we have today is a group of high tech suppliers selling to a group of low tech users. This is the tech gap.

DuPont had alliances with Xerox, Fuji, and Toyo and negotiations with the Warsaw Pact, NATO and the Cherokee Nation.

A friend of mine has a really cheap PC—it only does the work of ten bureaucrats.

I think I know why Microsoft and Apple want to get into fonts: revisions. New font revisions would add characters and re-design a few of them. Everything you ever set will have to be re-set.

Someone is programming a computer to read lips. I think it's George Bush. (You had to be there.)

To ward off thieves in New York, car owners have signs that say "No radios." I have a radio with a sign "No cars." The television has a sign that says "No sense" and my laser printer has one that states "No Souvenir."

My computer has a virus
Its bits have flown the coop
But I have just the cure
A disk of chicken soup

My friend said that after two months of computer dating they're ready for humans again.

Buzzwords

My new invention: the Buzzword Processor. Use it to create titillating word groups that seem to promise much but produce little. Summarize complex technologies with cute phrases. Sort of fore wordplay.

1970s
Word processing
1980s
Desktop publishing
1990s
Multimedia
2000s
4th dimension publishing

Buzzwords are fast food for thought.

Sign in a local computer store: "Buzzbull spoken here."

Some consultants believe that when they have coined a buzzword, they have solved a problem.

Buzzwords are a substitute for thinking.

Why are they called buzzwords? Because they attract flies.

The seminar had simultaneous translation for the buzzword impaired.

Buzzword: the immediate knowledge of something unencumbered by the process of thought.

I have discovered where there is an information black hole, where knowledge is sucked into oblivion, leaving only buzzwords and innocuous platitudes as a substitute for meaningful communications and action. It exists at the center of most conference tables.

Buzzwords: ideas have packaging too.

Most contracts are buzzword play.

Do Something Now

And so it was that all the computers in the world were interfaced into one giant network. All of the PCs from Dell to H-P to Apple to Compaq and IBM and all the clones and Macintoshes and laptops and luggables and desktops and minis and mainframes and super computers dedicated their combined power to solving one problem.

Every programmer who ever wrote code in Fortran and Cobol and Assembler and LISP and C and Basic and any other language that allowed machines to emulate human thought wrote software to solve one problem.

For input, all the recorded information of civilization was entered: science and art and history and politics and medicine and mathematics and astronomy and all the facts and data from all the libraries in all the world in every language spoken by man, past and present, to provide a database for solving one problem Scanners digitized every nook and cranny of the planet, it flora and fauna, transportation, cities, roads, parks, playgrounds, slums, apartments, and all the infrastructure that mankind has built for himself, to solve one problem.

To hold this information every floppy disk and hard disk and optical disk and tape drive and memory module was put on-line so that every piece of data was instantaneously accessible to solve this one problem.

And finally one person sat at an old Kaypro and typed:

HOW DO WE SAVE THE EARTH?

And the extraordinary computing power that had been assemble reviewed the sum total of all human existence, moving electrons frantically over circuits measured in light years, processing, comparing, evaluating data, and finally printing the answer to that one problem:

DO SOMETHING NOW.

No More Random Bits

My son wants to know why they can't have self-cleaning rooms, like self-cleaning ovens? I think we need self-cleaning kids. Or programmable kids who do exactly what their software instructs. Now that would be interpersonal computing.

The Pentagon wants to build a stealth blimp. It will deceive enemy radar into thinking it's a flying whale.

In this dream I'm the last person on earth with the last fax machine. Suddenly a page prints out. It's an ad for fax paper.

It wasn't so long ago that we all thought that paper tape was great. Some folks thought they were holes. I saw them as empty pixels.

What would it take to store all that mankind has learned since the dawn of time: optical disks, hard disks, mag tape, floppy disks? How about one punch card?

I have seen a lot of amateur typography and design since publishing came in, but I am not prepared for what it will look like in color.

My computer has a built-in anti theft approach. It's an Osborne.

Steve Jobs says that we no longer have Personal Computing. Now it's Interpersonal Computing. This means I might have a deep personal relationship with my machine. But if we split up, who gets custody of the disks?

Cyperspace is the name given to a branch of computing that can create a completely computer-generated, artificial world. Like TV.

You can then see, hear, and touch objects that only exist as computer data. You can do more than interact. You can go steady with your spreadsheet.

You could design a building with computer assisted drafting software and then walk through the artificial architecture. It's un-real estate.

At Boston's Computer Museum you can walk through a PC 50 times normal size—but that's real un-reality. Virtual reality is stealth un-reality. Like it really isn't there but you think it's there—akin to Social Security.

A teraflop computer is 1000 times faster than today's supercomputers, which are mere gigafloppy machines. Thus we make a quantum leap in computer processing speed from billions of operations per second to trillions of operations per second. Our government is the major user of supercomputing which goes to prove that fast machines don't make people faster.

Everyone blames the computer. Even congress says the computer did it. They have formed a committee (what else is new) to study the situation.

Another branch of computing concerns fuzzy logic, which lets computers deal with the area between yes and no, zero and one, and on and off. They have now programmed indecisiveness. At last, a computer that thinks like I do.

Apple Computer recently buried 2700 Lisa workstations in a Utah landfill. This is in preparation for the erection of a burial chamber for departing Apple executives who wish to go to the next world with products that didn't make it in this one.

One developer can now store 90mb of data on a 30mb disk. Can they get me into trousers with a 40" waist? Dream on.

Just before I die my life will probably pass before my eyes…in alphabetical order. All the way from A to B.

Or, my life will be stored on an optical disk and just before I go I will have to point to the button: "For more information, click here." And the screen will be blank.

Someday you'll have a demo disk of your life. Just my luck, mine will be on a 100K 8" floppy

Multimedia is MTV publishing.

They always precede the word multimedia with the word interactive. That is non-interactive multimedia? A book!

Can you recycle television programming? Sure, re-runs.

My monitor is on its last pixels. Sort of terminal terminal.

Heard of a sound bite. Multimedia is a sight bite.

When interfacing with strange ASCII for file conversion remember to practice safe HEX.

The designer graphical user interface: Gucci GUI (pronounced goochy gooey.) I think Hiawatha came from somewhere around there.

Seminar announcement I'd like to see

First Millennial Galactic
Non-conference Conference
Sponsored by no one
in particular
No date set or even planned
No speakers
Which reduces note taking and
audio-visual requirements
No charge
Credit cards accepted
Discount for early non-registration
Exhibits by firms with non-existent
vaporware products.
Conveniently located nowhere
An Amtrak stop
No phone listed
Non-existent fax
Ignored by over 20,000
Industry non-attendees.
Don't miss it!

This book is an example of textual harassment.

There are now more people over the age of 50 than teenagers in the United States. It just seems like there are more teenagers because they're a lot noisier.

I feel good finally being part of a real majority, but did it have to be old people?

Congress is a political in-action committee.

What do you call full animation, interactive, high-definition sound and video multimedia? Life

Bacon said "Reading makes a full man, conference a ready man, and writing an exact man." Multimedia makes a congressman.

Reading: close encounters of the word kind.

Reading is to the mind what exercise is to the body said Addison. My body may be a wreck but my mind looks like it's on steroids. A sweat band around my cerebellum?

I believe that print is the only secure repository of human knowledge. No matter what electronic medium you record today, it will be obsolete within five years. I defy any one of you to go out right now and find someone who can read an 8" Vydec floppy disk. What chance will you have 20 years from now with a VHS tape, a CD-ROM or any known magnetic disk. We will need media anthropologists to convert ancient media.

A recent issue of *Fortune* magazine had an article titled "America won't win till it reads more." Kids have calculators so they don't have to do arithmetic in their head; they have spelling checkers so they don't have to spell. They have grammar checkers so they don't have to organize their thoughts. Heck, why not replace the printed word with a flashy screenfull of transient information and create a real generation of couch potatoes?

We can't all work at McDonalds.

Goethe said that architecture was frozen music; if that is so, typography must be music for the eyes.

Then think of Souvenir as the Spike Jones of typefaces.

Electronic books are being released in many different formats: disks of different types, CD-ROMs, etc. At least with paper and print we have a standard that everyone can read without a battery-operated reader.

Of course, one should know how to read, no matter what the medium.

Steve Jobs once said that machines can increase human power. Mankind can use tools to equal or surpass the best of the animal kingdom. He said that the computer is a bicycle for our minds. When surrounded by a group of rogue elephants, I don't know if a bike is the tool I would want.

Computers are useless without people. Prove it for yourself: go up to the machine and tell it make a page. Without you, nothing happens. So the real question is: which one of you is the tool?

Man does not live by mouse alone.

For those of you who are really weird, there is now an inflatable PC.

Computers follow instructions exactly. In this respect they are totally unlike teenagers.

A guide to pronunciation
Dayter: common knowledge.
Day-tah: information
Dah-tuh; William F Buckley with a head cold.

Invertebratography: spineless typography

Today King Richard would have said "A mouse, a mouse, my kingdom for a mouse."

A messy user interface: gooey GUI.

Carlyle said that life is a gleam of time between two eternities. Today he would have said it was a mere sight and sound bite on some galactic broadcast.

PC Therapist III is an electronic psychiatrist. The program won an award by convincing experts that they were conversing with a real live person. If computers can truly mimic human thought processes and communication, why not automate Congress? The computer could make a speech, spell check it, set it in type, read it, and then correct its own errors, all instantly. Democratic computers would be Macs and Republican computers would probably be PCs. Independents would be clones.

Thinking Machines of Cambridge, MA has a new massively parallel processing computer with a massive price tag. It is being programmed to find a customer for itself.

The Library

There are certain memories that cause an emotional rush…when your scalp tingles or your eyes well up. Hopefully they are good memories like a wedding day or the birth of a child, or a graduation.

For me there is another one, and it may sound silly, but it was the day I got my first library card.

It all came back the other night when someone was talking about those days before television when radio was our primary medium. The person said they liked radio because the pictures were better.

And suddenly I was back in 1951 at the Brooklyn Public Library branch at Flatbush Avenue and Kings Highway. I recall that I had to have a note from my teacher and had to be able to sign my name in script. And I then had the most wonderful ticket anyone could ever have to travel in space and time.

I grabbed the first book I saw to check out. It was "A Tree Grows in Brooklyn" and I got an immediate frown from the librarian. Over the years I went from shelf to shelf looking through every book, scanning some, and checking out many. It was even my goal to read the entire Encyclopaedia Britannica but I lost interest somewhere around "I."

The words on those pages became images in my imagination. I didn't need a picture of the Nautilus or of Captain Nemo. I knew just what they looked like. Now we are at another generation of technology and human consciousness. Our kids have grown up in a more literal world where the image is the thing and the word is less important. Where you have to see it, not imagine it.

And we are being told about multimedia computing

There was a discussion between a group of technologists and a group of authors. The technologists pushed their vision of a world of video screens with access to databases and other information with sound and sight. "Look at all the information you have access to," said the technologists. "It's called a library," said the authors.

Computers and libraries are not enemies. From the computerized card catalog to the online information sources, I can see great synergy between the world of the printed book and the world of the pixel book.

My first reaction is to fight the whole idea of multimedia. Seeing kids playing with computers to learn their history or math just does not seem right to me. But I know there is a middle ground where the book and the TV set meet. For research purposes, the computer is a winner. There is no better way to search through data.

Although, I must say that using print sometimes leads to serendipitous discoveries.

I would rather see kids raised on print and then phased over to the computer. A front-page article in the *New York Times* reported that over the last decade, the sound bites used on TV news have gone from two minutes to less that 15 seconds. Life is transient enough.

But most of all, I don't like the idea of the electric book. The very idea of a machine between me and those words is a cultural shock. Reading requires that you concentrate and mentally repeat the words. This reinforces learning. The computer screen appears to engender less attention.

At one time, books were priced for the masses. Remember the first paperback books at a quarter and how shocked we were when they hit a buck. Now they are $6 or more for a paperback and over $24 for a hardcover book. Will the book on a disk be cheaper? Even so, you will still need a machine at a few hundred dollars or more to read it.

We are no longer pricing or providing information for the masses, but for a select intelligensia—those who can afford the computers and the digital appliances. Print is surely more democratic. *And the pictures are better.*

Save the planet Jupiter. It's too late to save Earth.

The Magellan space probe is on a search for artificial intelligence in the universe. It is programmed to avoid Washington, DC.

No one ever expected the Spanish imposition...

However, Apple says that the look and feel of the universe are too close to the Macintosh. Microsoft says that Windows is the universe.

I also think we should put DNA on a chip. Solid state genetics is the coming thing.

Darwin was wrong. Humanity did not evolve from less complex organisms, it has de-evolved from a highly intelligent being on its way to becoming pond scum.

Some of us may be closer to pond scum than others.

My life is more or less based on a true story. I'm living the abridged version this time around.

The human brain processes 3 million bytes of data per second. On a good day.

Intel should be working on a brain accelerator chip.

There are limits to free speech. You just can't yell "Souvenir" in a crowded typographer's meeting.

In your youth you had a mainframe. At your peak you had a mini. Now you must be content with a micro. CPUs have changed, haven't they?

Some folks would be right at home in artificial reality. I only visit it on weekends. It's cheaper.

High bandwidth: it's for phone lines, not waist lines.

Before there was time, nothing was ever late.

Desktop color: the unknowledgeable using the unspeakable in order to do the undoable. Unbelievable.

In the great cosmic scheme of things, everything is on time.

Remember how we once could communicate for the just the price of a postage stamp? Then we needed priority mail and air mail and now e-mail. Soon we will want our stuff faster than e-mail—sort of instantaneous universal consciousness, or hyper-zen communication.

Then each of us will need a hyper-zen code.

Computer crime is rampant. My PC has been holding up convenience stores at night.

The police know who it is. They have a mouse print on the gun.

Do you get the feeling that computer viruses are created by the same people who make those computer virus detectors? Nah!

I have seen the future and it isn't what it used to be.

And some day history will be a thing of the past.

My computer also suffers from premature calculation. It can only Lotus 1-2.

Its monitor is so old, it's gray and white.

It's a color monitor but I can't tell which one.

Running Head: just jiggle the handle.

What the text giveth, the footnote taketh away.

This is not reality. We are just a part of someone else's video game.

I used to be indecisive but now I'm not sure.

There's real reality which is really real and virtual reality, which is unreal. A virtual world does not exist. But you can still visit it. Like Disneyland.

Warning: The Surgeon General of the United States has determined that health maintenance organizations are dangerous to your health.

I think volunteers are overpaid.

My life is being kept secret by the government.

The U.S. Army has purchased a number of personal portable electronic reference systems for its field technicians. Each unit acquired from Reddy Information Systems consists of a belt-mounted DOS computer and CD-ROM player attached to earphones and a 1" eyeball level screen. Price tag is $4,995 each. This system let the maintenance technician work with both hands while listening to instructions or looking at schematics.

Think of it as a $4,995 book. I'll wait for the paper book version.

What we really need is a program that converts glitzy graphics back into tables of alphanumeric information. Graphs are great but data is greater.

And I'll bet you a dollar that this electronic system comes with an operating manual. Or at least a sheet of instructions. (Actually, it does. Long live paper.)

This device tells me one thing: invest in the Energizer Bunny.

Math illiteracy affects eight out of every five people.

A related episode: I was on the Amtrak Metroliner from New York to Washington watching a young fellow (they all seem younger lately) play with his Macintosh laptop computer. He was learning to use Microsoft Word...and the Word manual weighed more than the computer.

Hypertext is being hyped as information in all four dimensions. This means that a computer can actually access data that is backward or forward in time. You can read memos that you write tomorrow, today, and change what you predicted yesterday to match the results of tomorrow. This is the perfect tool for the corporate office. You can get your work done yesterday by people who were out then but will start today because their off tomorrow.

They had started to build the super conducting super collider in Texas. It would have accelerated sub atomic particles to the speed of light. It was being designed by the same people who design roller coaster rides at amusement parks.

In another time and place Abraham Lincoln would have written the Gettysburg Address on the back of a Toshiba portable.

Smart Paper

Paper is said to have the highest impedance factor in the eye-brain connection. This means that we can get information from paper faster than from a TV screen which is shooting millions of pixels at us.

I read that Xerox is introducing a concept called "smart paper." Batteries are not included.

In fact, paper is not included.

If paper were smart, it would be currency.

If a single sheet of paper is smart, and entire book must be brilliant.

Then think about how very smart a library is.

Are ledger-sized sheets of paper smarter than standard-sized paper? Is bigger smarter?

Like high IQ paper?

We could even have smart toilet paper.

If it were so smart, it wouldn't be toilet paper.

And dumb paper is a supermarket tabloid.

Smart paper should correct its own typos.

On the other hand, I'm not thrilled with the idea of working with paper smarter than I am.

Paper that thinks. There's a concept for you.

How about people who think?

A blank sheet isn't smart, just silent.

We are all pixel watchers.

Now they want to introduce paperless fax.

But if there is no paper, how can it be fax?

The paper companies will then introduce fax-less paper. Eventually we will have paperless paper.

It will be used for stealth documents.

But not a paperless bathroom.

Imagine a world without paper. Politicians would have nothing to shred.

I once said that there would be a paperless office when there was a paperless bathroom. Now I read that the Japanese have developed an electronic toilet. I don't know about you, but there are some places I just don't want technology messing around.

Paper can be lethal. I got a memo saying my job had been terminated.

Electronic paper has an electrical cord.

Random Bits? Nah!

It will start innocently with voice mail and then voice input. There was something about talking to a machine that bothered me. Talking into a Dictaphone didn't. Talking into the clown's nose at McDonald's doesn't. Even voice mail was acceptable to some extent. Along comes voice input and conversing with a machine now puts it on an equal footing with humanity, with me. It will not be long before the machines become more demanding. I can imagine them saying "Please repeat that; I don't understand you." Then they will make editorial comments. Then they will make snide remarks. They will eventually protest for equality. Then they will want the vote. (This will allow them to more accurately predict the outcome of an election.) And then, in some future yet to come, they will be dictating to us.

Fat free, sodium free, sugar free—do you often feel that some people should be labeled "intelligence free."

The Library of Congress is the largest repository human knowledge in the world. So close to Congress yet so far.

Three congressmen are actually known to have overdue books on their library card.

Your sister could go steady with a toaster.

There will be billboards that proclaim"machines are people too." Washing machines will be in therapy because they feel inferior.

To machines, God is Cray supercomputer.

What do you call a Cray with nuclear weapons? Sir!

Amigas only believe in Atari.

Machines will write books (I think they author romance novels now), edit them, produce them, and then optically read them.

Machines are really taking over. I can see where it is all going—people standing by parking meters as their cars are shopping at the mall.

This is what will happen if we become electronic voyeurs and live life vicariously. Instead of doing life, we are playing Nintendo versions of it.

With virtual reality we will become the machine and the machine will become us.

Sort of a humachine.

Q: What do you call an unemployed machine?
A: Scrap.

Cogito ergo sum, baby

The real purpose of a darkroom is to keep the dark in.

In the latest episode of "As The World Kerns," Lance decides to become the world's first proofreader to work with a blindfold. His first job is the Federal Budget proposal and he sees through it immediately.

Reading: Close Encounters of the Word Kind

Based on a ideas expressed by a past president of R.R. Donnelley.

In a corner of a printing plant in Illinois, there stands a giant printing press that once ran night and day, producing sets of encyclopedias that would line the walls of American homes. Today, it stands silently. It will never run again on a regular basis.

Overnight, the preferred medium for encyclopedias switched from print to CD-ROM.

People used to pay more than $2,000 for a printed encyclopedia. Now they can buy a CD-ROM encyclopedia for $40 —or get it free with the purchase of almost any family computer.

They say that multimedia gives you virtually unlimited access to information. With it you can learn just about anything.

I felt the same way when I first learned how to use a library.

But CD-ROM publishing is a paradox. The CD-ROM standard has gone through six speed changes, and it is about to be wiped out by DVD. It's not that we do not have standards; we have too many standards. The pioneers who bought in early at 1X and 2X or even 4X need to upgrade to 12X or 24X or DVD-ROM.

My computer has magnetic hard disk storage, internal and external, floppy disk, both 3-1/2 and 5-1/4, 44 and 88 mb Syquest, magneto optical, Zip and Jaz drives, Bernoulli, CD-ROM, multi-gigabyte hard drives and DAT tape.

I have unlisted SCSI addresses.

In my garage I also have 78, 45 and 33 and 1/3 records, cassette tapes, cartridges and now compact disks. Some of you have Beta systems. Soon all VHS will be replaced by digital video disk. There's nothing wrong with being a pioneer.

The definition of pioneer no longer deals with arrows: a pioneer is someone with a big garage.

A future occupation may be data archeologist.

I have seen the Dead Sea Scrolls and it is quite a thrill to see 5,000 year old writings. If they were the Dead CD-ROMs, forget it.

CD-ROM publishers are unique. They count the copies they give away in their sales. Does General Motors know about this? They could triple their sales overnight

Much of what I see is multi-mediocrity. But the potential is enormous. When it is good, it is mindboggling. When it is bad, it is the norm.

I was looking at a book from the 15th century the other day. No computer. No CD-ROM reader. Just a pair of old eyes—with bifocals however. All these new publishing approaches seem to restrict rather than expand access to information. We are creating an information elite, sort of an artificial intelligensia. Paper and television are the media to reach mass markets.

The company that finds a way to combine them will inherit the earth.

My market used to be publishing and ink on paper products. Today we have printing companies who maintain databases, printers who stamp CD-ROMs, printers who produce multimedia. And by the way, they also put ink on paper or board or plastic or foil. Last year R.R. Donnelley paid more for disks of all kinds than they did for paper of all kinds. What then is a printer? What then is the printing industry?

There is a theorem of the digital revolution known as the cannibal principle. It holds that integrated circuits absorb the functions of discrete electronic components, incorporate them into a single new chip and give back those functions free. You get something for nothing.

A business built on digital technology acts in much the same way; it absorbs the functions of other businesses and gives them back free to the consumer. The customer pays less and gets more. The digital supplier gains a new revenue stream. And scores of traditional suppliers lose everything. The results: a win-win-lose world.

In this new world, many traditional businesses might as well have bull's-eyes painted on them. They are the targets of someone's cannibal-principle strategy. Those who say print is dead do so in newsletters. The Wall Street Journal described printing as a "sunset industry" a while back. They had to say it in print for anyone to know.

The key is not to doggedly defend an indefensible position in paper publishing but to look at the entire book publishing marketplace and search for an opportunity to change the rules. Book publishers often miss the market by printing too many copies or too few. The front-end costs of printing were so high that a publisher could not afford to print a few and come back later to print a few more if the demand warranted it.

So my industry developed a concept for taking a publisher's content in digital form and using digital processes to print only as many copies as the publisher needed in the short term. On-demand printing. No inventory. No warehouse. Just-in-time manufacturing.

How do we know we're right? The answer hinges on how we perceive digital technology. Do we believe it will continue to expand its influence in the marketplace? If we believe in a digital future, then our best bet is to pattern ourselves after what is real about digital technology.

We used to make changes in business according to this command:

> Ready. Aim. Fire!
> Today, the command has to be:
> Fire. Aim. Fire. Aim. Fire. Aim!

You fire in order to aim. Fire a burst. See what happens. Make corrections. Fire another burst. Build speed into everything you do and measure yourself against the speed of the world around you.

When the medium of choice in the encyclopedia business shifted to CD-ROM, there was nothing comparable in our experience. The velocity, conclusiveness and irreversibility of the shift were unprecedented.

It has been said that digital technology eats everything and tramples anyone who tries to oppose it. I believe that understates the case. You don't have to oppose digital technology to be trampled; innocent bystanders will be flattened, too. There is no neutrality in the Digital Revolution. You must become a digital revolutionary or risk losing everything.

At the start of the French Revolution they tore down the Bastille. At the start of the Information Revolution I tore up a rather vicious memo.

Take the Internet, please.

In dealing with a medium that has gone, by some estimates, from 30 million users to 65 million in a year (now 80 million), researchers are finding their subject an elusive target.

People with high school education or less make up 52 percent of the adult American population but only 19 percent of Internet users, and those with at least a college degree make up 22 percent of the adult American population but 53 percent of the online population.

Even though the largest proportion of Web users is composed of people in their 20s and 30s, the proportion of people older than 65 has increased sharply since 1995. The research shows that 1 percent of people in that age group had logged on in 1995, but that 6 percent used the Internet in the recent surveys.

Grandma is on the Web.

Although the survey did not ask whether people accessed the Internet at home, at work or in a public setting, demographic gaps are closing because of better public Internet access through libraries, schools and community centers.

Today Internet access rests with those earning $67,000 a year or more. Just as the book and other forms of print became more democratic, so must Internet access. Gutenberg's invention made lead more valuable than gold because virtually everyone understood what print could do. No one really knows what the so-called information superhighway can do.

We are re-wiring America with fiber optic cable.

For print to be displaced as the primary means of communication, you must replace it with as pervasive a communication channel. Cable TV is not. Broadcast TV is close. The Internet is not even close. It is more or less electronic graffiti on the info highway.

In fact, there is no one medium that would allow you to reach the mass of humans on this planet. Well, yes there is—paper.

Paper is a one-dimensional medium in a multi-media world. It is friendly and portable. Someone asked what if paper could talk. If it talked too much could I shut it up with Scotch tape. Would tinted paper have an accent? Ledger stock talk with a deep voice? Will other stationery items also become verbose? I can picture someone returned a bad ream of paper "It mumbles."

The challenge of today's technology is not to make people computer literate but to make computers people literate.

"Surf the web" says a lot about people with attention deficit disorder. The Internet could be a network of networks with millions of people with short attention spans and too much idle time searching for the ultimate diversion. Most Internet users are white males under 24 and popular sites involve erotica. The reason: no staples.

The Internet is like CB radio, only you have to type. How do you make money on the Internet: This guy ran magazine ads for years telling you how he got rich and for $20 he would tell you the secret. I sent the 20 bucks and got a booklet telling me to run magazine ads on how I got rich by charging $20 for the same information.

More people will make more money telling other people how to make money than real users will, trying to make money by actually doing something. Another oxymoron: net profits. Some say cyberspace is a parallel universe. Get a parallel life.

A major urban problem: the home page less.

It started with the personal computer. We needed more data for decisionmaking so computers were the answer. Then computers generated more data than we could deal with so we needed hypertext and intelligent databases to find the information faster. So now we need to use the computer to find information because the computer creates more information than we can deal with.

Marshall McLuhan was a great thinker. He summed up his views on the effects of media in the maxim "the medium is the message"—the way we acquire information affects us more than the information itself.

McLuhan believed that television has a profound impact on children not because of what is on it, but because of what is in it. Its mosaic pattern of dots of light, its lack of detail, its motion and sound, and the fact that the light comes at the viewer—all these things make television-watching an aural and visual experience, he said, and far more deeply involving for a child than reading a book.

He contended that print, by involving only the visual sense, and by presenting information in small bits, one by one, separated thought from feeling and led to the fragmentation of knowledge. It enabled Western man to specialize and to mechanize, but it also led, he said, to "alienation from their other senses."

He believed that electronic media, by showing what was happening on the other side of the world, were creating a global electronic village in which books would become obsolete.

To describe the effects of different media, McLuhan used the terms "hot" and "cool." A hot medium was one that "allows less participation than a cool one, as a lecture makes for less participation than a seminar, and a book for less than a dialogue."

Despite his own choice of a hot medium—books—in which to express himself, McLuhan was considered by some as an oracle of the electronic age. Wired magazine lists him as "patron saint." Others accused him of being a confused phrasemonger or an outright charlatan. Wired magazine only makes money in print.

One of his books discussed the effects on Western European culture of the invention of movable type in the 15th century. McLuhan proposed that the resulting dominance of print accounted for linear development in musical and serial thinking, in mathematics and the sciences.

As print superseded oral communication the eye superseded the ear as the primary sensory organ.

But with the 20th-century electronic age, he said, mankind returned to certain tribal ways because the world had become "a global village." Electronic media, especially television, re-distributed and heightened sensory awareness to such a degree that previous separation of thought and action was significantly reduced. Electronic circuitry, he also said, made human behavior less isolated and more conformist.

But he did not live long enough to see the Internet as a challenge to television.

But at the end: "The book is a very special form of communication," he told a convention of the American Booksellers Association. "It is unique and it will persist."

The Computer Restaurant

Server: Hi, my name is Bill and I'll be your Server. What is the problem?
Customer: There's a fly in my soup!
Server: I never heard of that.
Customer: Well, there is a fly in my soup.
Server: Are you sure it's a fly.
Customer: Yes, it is a fly.
Server: Try the soup again, maybe the fly won't be there this time.
Customer: It's still there.
Server: Maybe it's the way you're using the soup; try eating it with a fork.
Customer: The fly is still there.
Server: Maybe the soup is incompatible with the bowl; what kind of bowl are you using?
Customer: A soup bowl.
Server: Hmmm, that should work. Maybe it's a configuration problem; how was the bowl set up?
Customer: You brought it to me on a saucer; what has that to do with the fly in my soup?
Server: Can you remember everything you did before you noticed the fly in your soup?
Customer: I sat down and ordered the Soup of the Day.
Server: Have you considered upgrading to the latest Soup of the Day?
Customer: You have more than one Soup of the Day each day?
Server: Yes, the Soup of the Day is changed every hour.
Customer: What is the Soup of the Day now?
Server: The current Soup of the Day is tomato.
Customer: Fine. Bring me the tomato soup and the check. I'm running late now.
Server leaves and returns with another bowl of soup and the check.
Server: Here you are, Sir. The soup and your check.
Customer: This is potato soup.
Server: Yes, the tomato soup wasn't ready yet.
Customer: Well, I'm so hungry now, I'll eat anything.
Server leaves.
Customer: There's a gnat in my soup!

Boot Camp for the Paper Police
Only Wimps Read Books

It has recently come to my attention that many of you have developed serious book habits. As a drill instructor in information technology, I have seen first hand the grisly damage caused by the use of books, the hollow, vacant staring eyes of the hardcore reader, lying face down in a pile of papers in the corner of a public library. It's not a pretty sight.

Statistics show that most Americans are well acquainted with the dangers of books and wisely avoid their use, but I've even seen ostensibly responsible adults urging the naive and innocent youth of our nation to indulge their lust for knowledge in the most wanton and irresponsible manner possible, even publicly encouraging trips to libraries, reading books at night, even periodicals and journal articles. And never a word of warning, to advise these vulnerable youngsters of the wickedness, the lurking danger in these books.

Don't you folks see what happens to "readers"? It doesn't matter what you read—even a "pamphlet" can spark your interest, and once you're interested in something, it's all over; you'll be a reader for life, quickly moving on to heavier stuff. Eventually, you might even end up reading Homer. And not Simpson.

Unfortunately, books have thoroughly saturated the very structures of our society. But the Bible reassures us that eventually righteousness shall prevail, and *we will win the war on readers!* And so shall it end, when we return the land to righteousness, severely restrict the use of dangerous books, and burn those particularly damaging tracts which cannot be responsibly used by anyone.

I know the skeptical among you may be thinking, "What a hypocrite! He works for the printing industry, he admits to having read the Bible. He's a reader himself!" And all of that is true, but the crucial difference is that *the bible is not really a book!*

Yes, it has many similar characteristics of a book, but unlike harmful books like the *Hobbit* and *Huck Finn* (which should be banned everywhere) the Bible is far less likely to get you "interested." Most people read the Bible for its righteousness, not for its content. With responsible use, the Bible can be read safely without really causing interest or enlightenment. Indeed, the Bible can hardly be characterized as a recreational book; it's very hard to get even a giggle out of it, and most people never laugh when reading the Bible.

Books should only be read in moderation, if at all, under the guidance and care of a professional. We should all look out for one another: if you see a reader on the street, report them to the authorities at once; if caught early enough, some readers can be rehabilitated and reintegrated into society.

And if someone gives you a book, or even suggests that you read a book, JUST SAY NO! Support the fight for de-literization. This country will be much safer and tidier when we've finally rounded up all the book dealers and thrown them in jail and seized their illicit private stashes of books.

Alphabetic amnesia: has an illness resulting from too many acronyms.

From the Mount

Then the Prophet took His disciples up the mountain and gathered them around Him.

He taught them saying, "Blessed are the poor in spirit for theirs is the kingdom of heaven. Blessed are the meek."

Blessed are they that mourn. Blessed are they who thirst after righteousness. Blessed are they who are persecuted.

Blessed are they who suffer. Be glad and rejoice for your reward is great in heaven.

"Remember what I am telling you."

Then Simon Peter said, "Do we have to write this down?"

And Andrew said, "Are we supposed to know this?"

And James said, "Will we be tested on it?"

And Bartholomew said, "Do we have to turn this in?"

And John said, "The other disciples didn't have to learn this."

And the other disciples likewise. Then one of the Pharisees who was present asked to see the Prophet's lesson plan and inquired of the Prophet His distance learning goals and terminal objectives in the cognitive domain.

And the Prophet wept.

Fearless Predictions

"Computers in the future may weigh no more than 1.5 tons."
—Popular Mechanics, forecasting the relentless march of science, 1949.

I guess they never saw a Kaypro.

"I think there is a world market for maybe five computers."
—Thomas Watson, Chairman of IBM, 1943.

But they have to be really big computers.

"I have traveled the length and breadth of this country and talked with the best people, and I can assure you that data processing is a fad that won't last out the year."
—The editor in charge of business books for Prentice Hall, 1957

But what year was he talking about?

"But what...is it good for?"
—Engineer at the Advanced Computing Systems Division of IBM, 1968, commenting on the microchip.

Boy, did they change their tune.

"There is no reason anyone would want a computer in their home."
—Ken Olson, president, chairman and founder of Digital Equipment Corp., 1977

And now DEC is part of Compaq.

"This 'telephone' has too many shortcomings to be seriously considered as a means of communication. The device is inherently of no value to us."
—Western Union internal memo, 1876.

Boy, did they have a wrong number.

"The wireless music box has no imaginable commercial value. Who would pay for a message sent to nobody in particular?"—David Sarnoff's associates in response to his urgings for investment in the radio in the 1920s.

And what did radio give us? Rush Limbaugh and Howard Stern.

"The concept is interesting and well-formed, but in order to earn better than a 'C,' the idea must be feasible."—A Yale University management professor in response to Fred Smith's paper proposing reliable overnight delivery service. (Smith went on to found Federal Express Corp.)

The professor did not absolutely, positively get it.

"Who the hell wants to hear actors talk?"
—H.M. Warner, Warner Brothers, 1927.

But what about Marcel Marceau?

"I'm just glad it'll be Clark Gable who's falling on his face and not Gary Cooper."—Gary Cooper on his decision not to take the leading role in "Gone With The Wind."

Frankly my dear Gary, I don't give a damn.

"A cookie store is a bad idea. Besides, the market research reports say America likes crispy cookies, not soft and chewy cookies like you make."—Response to Debbi Fields' idea of starting Mrs. Fields' Cookies.

And now she is in the chips.

"We don't like their sound, and guitar music is on the way out."—Decca Recording Co. rejecting the Beatles, 1962

Ah, the sound of foot in mouth.

"Heavier-than-air flying machines are impossible."
—Lord Kelvin, president, Royal Society, 1895.

They still are.

"If I had thought about it, I wouldn't have done the experiment. The literature was full of examples that said you can't do this."—Spencer Silver on the work that led to the unique adhesives for 3M "Post-It" Notepads.

A sticky that isn't really sticky but is just sticky enough.

"So we went to Atari and said, "Hey, we've got this amazing thing, even built with some of your parts, and what do you think about funding us? Or we'll give it to you. We just want to do it. Pay our salary, we'll come work for you." And they said, 'No.' So then we went to Hewlett-Packard, and they said, 'Hey, we don't need you. You haven't got through college yet.'"—Apple Computer Inc. founder, Steve Jobs, on attempts to get Atari and H-P interested in his and Steve Wozniak's personal computer.

Imagine Steve Jobs as an employee.

"Professor Goddard does not know the relation between action and reaction and the need to have something better than a vacuum against which to react. He seems to lack the basic knowledge ladled out daily in high schools."
—1921 *New York Times* editorial about Robert Goddard's revolutionary rocket work.

He should have aimed the rocket at the Times building.

"You want to have consistent and uniform muscle development across all of your muscles? It can't be done. It's just a fact of life. You just have to accept inconsistent muscle development as an unalterable condition of weight training."—Response to Arthur Jones, who solved the "unsolvable" problem by inventing Nautilus.

He never saw the ThighMaster.

"Drill for oil? You mean drill into the ground to try and find oil? You're crazy."—Drillers who Edwin L. Drake tried to enlist to his project to drill for oil in 1859.

We all know that oil comes from cans.

"Stocks have reached what looks like a permanently high plateau."—Irving Fisher, Professor of Economics, Yale University, 1929.

There was no Alan Greenspan back then.

"Airplanes are interesting toys but of no military value."—Marechal Ferdinand Foch, Professor of Strategy, Ecole Superieure de Guerre.

Curse you, Red Baron.

"Everything that can be invented has been invented."—Charles H. Duell, Commissioner, U.S. Office of Patents, 1899.

And everyone who can be born has been born.

"Louis Pasteur's theory of germs is ridiculous fiction."—Pierre Pachet, Professor of Physiology at Toulouse, 1872.

He never read "The Andromeda Strain."

"The abdomen, the chest, and the brain will forever be shut from the intrusion of the wise and humane surgeon."
—Sir John Eric Ericksen, British surgeon, appointed Surgeon-Extraordinary to Queen Victoria 1873.

He went on to invent laser circumcision.

"640K ought to be enough for anybody."— Bill Gates, 1981.

You don't have to be right to be rich.

Murphy Was Here

Whenever a system becomes completely defined, some darn fool discovers something which either abolishes the system or expands it beyond all recognition.

Anything that can go wrong will go wrong. Right on.

It is impossible to make anything foolproof because fools are so ingenious.

If everything seems to be going well, you have obviously overlooked something.

Left to themselves, things tend to go from bad to worse.

The legibility of a copy is inversely proportional to its importance.

Things get worse under pressure.

Everything goes wrong all at once.

Matter will be damaged in direct proportion to its value.

Solutions breed problems.

Things are under pressure all the time.

You never run out of things that can go wrong.

Logic is a systematic method of coming to the wrong conclusion with confidence.

Technology is dominated by those who manage what they do not understand.

A meeting is an event at which minutes are kept and hours are lost.

The first myth of management is that it exists.

More Murphy

Any computer design will contain at least one part which is quickly obsoleted, two parts which are unobtainable, and three parts which are still under development.

A failure will not appear until a unit has passed final inspection.

New systems generate new problems.

Any program, when running, is obsolete.

Any sufficiently advanced technology is indistinguishable from magic.

A computer makes as many mistakes in two seconds as 20 humans working 20 years make.

Some people manage by the book, even though they don't know who wrote the book or even what book.

The function of the design engineer is to make things difficult for the fabricator and impossible for the serviceman.

To spot the expert, pick the one who predicts the job will take the longest and cost the most.

After all is said and done, a lot more is said than done.

Computers are unreliable, but humans are even more unreliable. Any system which depends on human reliability is unreliable.

The only perfect science is hindsight.

If it's not in the computer, it doesn't exist.

If there is a possibility of several things going wrong the one that will cause the most damage will be the one to go wrong.

Any simple theory will be worded in the most complicated way.

Build a system that even a fool can use and only a fool will want to use it.

The degree of technical competence is inversely proportional to the level of management.

The Cyber Family

Do you try to enter a password on the microwave?

Have you played solitaire with a real deck of cards in years.

Do you have a list of 15 phone numbers to reach your family of three?

Do you email your son in his room to tell him that dinner is ready, and he emails you back "What's for dinner?"

Does your daughter sells Girl Scout Cookies via her Web site?

Does every commercial on television have a web-site address at the bottom of the screen?

Did you buy a computer and a week later it is out of date and now sells for half the price you paid?

Is the concept of using real money, instead of credit or debit, to make a purchase is foreign to you?

The Computer Did It

A programmer is someone who fixes things that aren't broken.

A mainframe: the biggest PC peripheral available.

Any sufficiently advanced bug is indistinguishable from a feature.

Artificial Intelligence: Making computers behave like they do in the movies.

Best file compression around: "DEL *.*" = 100% compression

Capt'n! The spellchecker kinna take this abuse!

Computers are useless. They can only give you answers.
—Pablo Picasso

Computers are only human.

Computers make very fast, very accurate mistakes.

Upgrade: Take old bugs out, put new ones in.

Disinformation is not as good as datinformation.

Earth is 98% full...please delete anyone you can.

Error: Keyboard not attached. Press F1 to continue.

Hit any user to continue.

Honey, I Formatted the Kid!

I haven't lost my mind; it's backed up on tape somewhere.

I hit the CTRL key but I'm still not in control!

You might have mail.

If a train station is where the train stops, what is a work station?

If the pen is mightier than the sword, and a picture is worth a thousand words, how dangerous is a FAX?

Justify my text? I'm sorry but it has no excuse.

Multitasking: Screwing up several things at once.

Nobody has ever, ever, EVER learned all of WordPerfect.

I'm not a computer nerd; merely a techno-weenie.

Nothing is 100% certain, bug free or IBM compatible.

One picture is worth 1K words.

Press any key to continue or any other key to quit.

Sorry...my mind has a few bad sectors.

Those who can't write, write help files.

Toto, I don't think we're in DOS anymore...

WYGIWYD—What you got is what you deserved.

WYTYSYDG—What you thought you saw, you didn't get.

Signs You've Had Too Much of the 90s

22. Cleaning up the dining area means getting the Taco Bell bags out of the back seat of your car.
21. Your reason for not staying in touch with your family is that they do not have e-mail.
20. Keeping up with sports entails adding ESPN's homepage to your bookmarks.
19. You have a "to do list" that includes entries for lunch and bathroom breaks and they are usually the ones that never get crossed off.
18. You faxed your Christmas list to your family.
17. Pick up lines now include a reference to liquid assets and capital gains.
16. You consider 2nd day air delivery painfully slow.
15. You assume the question to valet park you BMW or not is rhetorical.
14. You refer to your dining room table as the flat filing cabinet.
13. Your idea of being organized is multiple colored Post-It notes.
12. Your grocery list has been on your refrigerator so long some of the products don't even exist any more.
11. You lecture the neighborhood kids selling lemonade on ways to re-engineer.
10. You get all excited when it's Saturday and you can wear sweats to work.
9. You refer to the tomatoes grown in your garden as deliverables.
8. You find you really need Powerpoint to explain what you do for a living.
7. You normally eat out of vending machines and at the most expensive restaurant in town within the same week.
6. You think that "progressing an action plan" and "calendarizing a project" are acceptable English phrases.
5. You know the people at airport hotels better than you know your next door neighbors.
4. You ask your friends to "think out of the box" when making Friday night plans.
3. You think Einstein would have been more effective had he put his ideas into a matrix.

2. You think a "half-day" means leaving at 5 o'clock.
1. You hear most of your jokes via e-mail instead of in person

After a past scandal at the Pentagon

Now here's a pretty mess
Now here's a pretty mess
  The Pentagon has got a scandal
  A bigger stew than it can handle
Nothing could be less
Nothing could be less
  Defense contractors under scrutiny
  Navy, Air Force brass near mutiny
All are in distress
All are in distress
  Wiretaps are quite revealing
  Of the wheeling and the dealing
It finally hit the press
It finally hit the press
  All those billions out for biddin'
  Some got spent and some got hidden
They cannot find the rest
They cannot find the rest
  Consultants and contractors lie
  Investigated by the FBI
Eventually to confess
Eventually to confess
  Ollie North did jump with glee
  "At least this time it isn't me"
That's into such a mess

God

God hired one of those big New York ad agencies to handle public relations since some of those evangelists and Ayatollahs were giving Him a bad name. The first meeting did not go well. The creative director wanted to portray God as an old philosopher. He was told that God is ageless, transcending time and place for eternities upon eternities. Then the art director wanted a photo shoot. He was told that God is the reality of heart and soul and not visible or even understandable in earthly terms. The chief copywriter wanted a bio. He was told that God was the creator and destroyer of universes, supreme being, and initiator of the cosmos and all things in it. He said that was kind of skimpy. The account executive summed it up "We have an invisible timeless entity with no evidence of existence who wants to be portrayed on more favorable terms." That's right, he was told. "Well, we did it with George W. Bush."

Pat Robertson has announced that if elected to the White House he will name God as his vice president. God has said that He wants real power and is holding out for owner of the *New York Yankees*.

God should start a newsletter...with a discount for an eternal subscription.

In the beginning was the buzzword and it begat the consultant who begat more buzzwords and more consultants. God should never have begun the begat.

There always seems to be another study by another consulting group that proves how vast the market is. It has been 30 years for my involvement and I haven't seen that big jump on the chart. Bean counters scare me. Gallup once said he could prove the existence of God statistically. All Moses needed was a burning bush.

Someone said that making jokes about God was sacreligious. Well, God has a sense of humor. Look at the aardvark and the dodo and even republicans.

Televangelists and others get messages from God. All I get is a busy signal. I have this feeling that if Moses was going to receive the Ten Commandments today, God would fax them. Do Group IV facsimile machines run granite?

Theologians have discovered that there is a Computer God, an omnipotent, omnipresent and galactic multi-tasking supreme CPU with an eternity of RAM and a limitless universe of real time on-line storage, that created data processing in its own image. Prayers are directed through the AOL bulletin board. Computer atheists believe that data processing life began with single-bit microchips born in the primordial sludge who evolved over the millennia and that the missing link is actually the TRS-80. Computer agnostics don't really care either way but back up their disk files every 30 seconds.

Archaeologists have discovered that Antarctica, when viewed from above, has the notation "This continent intentionally left blank." God may be getting ready for an update.

God created the universe on a genesis processor, stored it on a galactic floppy (the rings of Saturn are really for data) and printed it out in six days on an ultra-reality wholly holographic printer. He would have done it in less time but he wanted high resolution, perhaps higher resolution than we deserve.

Timothy Leary once wrote in the Boston Computer Society Update that the global religion of the 21st century will be called Higher Intelligence and that God will be the designer of the master program that runs the universe. Leary, who espoused the use of LSD in the Sixties was in the process of discovering the hallucinogenic power of oat bran before he died. He may find that Heaven is a letdown.

The United States Bureau of Engraving is thinking of printing bar coding on our paper currency to foil forgers and counterfeiters. The motto will then change to "In God we scan."

My latest ambition! To be in charge of research and development for God. I know I could have helped with the design of the universe. I think we need a lower-cost model for the mass market, maybe with fewer planets and a better user interface.

I wonder if God uses UNIX?

God created the world in six days. He could have done it in less but the documentation wasn't ready.

www.desertisland.com

An ambitious yuppie finally decided to take a vacation. He booked himself on a Caribbean cruise and proceeded to have the time of his life. Until the boat sank. The man found himself swept up on the shore of an island with no other people, no supplies...nothing. Only bananas and coconuts.

After about four months, he is lying on the beach one day when the most gorgeous woman he has ever seen rows up to him. In disbelief, he asks her, "Where did you come from? How did you get here?"

"I rowed from the other side of the island," she says. "I landed here when my cruise ship sank."

"Amazing," he says. "You were really lucky to have a rowboat wash up with you."

"Oh, this?" replies the woman. "I made the rowboat out of material I found on the island; the oars were whittled from gum tree branches; I wove the bottom from palm branches; and the sides and stern came from a Eucalyptus tree."

"But— but, that's impossible," stutters the man. "You had no tools or hardware. How did you manage?"

"Oh, that was no problem," replies the woman. "On the south side of the island, there is a very unusual strata of alluvial rock exposed. I found if I fired it to a certain temperature in my kiln, it melted into forgeable ductile iron. I used that for tools and used the tools to make the hardware."

The guy is stunned. "Let's row over to my place, " she says.

After a few minutes of rowing, she docks the boat at a small wharf. As the man looks onto shore, he nearly falls out of the boat. Before him is a stone walk leading to an exquisite bungalow painted in blue and white.

While the woman ties up the rowboat with an expertly woven hemp rope, the man can only stare ahead, dumbstruck.

As they walk into the house, she says casually "It's not much, but I call it home. Sit down and relax please; would you like to have a drink?"

"No, no thank you," he says, still dazed. "Can't take any more coconut juice."

"It's not coconut juice," the woman replies. "I have a still. How about a Piña Colada?"

Trying to hide his continued amazement, the man accepts, and they sit down on her couch to talk. After they have exchanged their stories, the woman announces, "I'm going to slip into something more comfortable. Would you like to take a shower and shave? There is a razor upstairs in the cabinet in the bathroom."

No longer questioning anything, the man goes into the bathroom. There, in the cabinet, is a razor made from a bone handle. Two shells honed to a hollow ground edge are fastened on to its end inside of a swivel mechanism.

"This woman is amazing," he muses. "What next?"

When he returns, she greets him wearing nothing but vines—strategically positioned—and smelling faintly of gardenias. She beckons for him to sit down next to her. "Tell me," she begins, suggestively, slithering closer to him, "We've been out here for a really long time. You've been lonely. There's something I'm sure you really feel like doing right now, something you've been longing for all these months? You know... "

She stares into his eyes. He can't believe what he's hearing:

"You mean—?", he swallowed excitedly,"—I can really check my e-mail from here?"

Politics

Labels are imprecise. Liberals take from the rich and give to the poor. Conservatives take from the poor and give to the rich. Middle-of-the-roaders take money from one pocket and put it in the other. The problem with all politicians is that they always take from someone to give to someone else. Do we really need a middleman?

Last year Elvis had one of the highest incomes in the United States. Evidently death does not affect earnings potential. No wonder that living people cannot find jobs. They have even found dead people receiving Social Security. I say we should find jobs for them. They would probably work faster than some bureaucrats.

A Stereotypical Guide

A conservative spends money on defense.
A liberal spends money on social services.
A conservative wants less government.
A liberal wants more government.

Therefore:

A liberal conservative wants to arm the poor.
A conservative liberal wants the poor to arm themselves.
A liberal liberal wants the poor to practice passive resistance.
A conservative conservative wants the poor to fight in Bosnia.

Politics is just like printing technology. In politics there are almost a dozen competitors for your vote but only to or three that matter. In technology there are over a dozen competitors for your order and only two or three that matter.

In politics they will tell you anything to get your vote. In technology they will do almost anything to get your order. In politics one person gets elected. In technology, one system gets selected.

In politics they get four years in office. In technology you get four years in hock.

In politics they become elder statesman. In technology they become consultants.

With Apologies to Gilbert & Sullivan

I've got a little list, I've got a little list
Of a society of scoundrels who never would be missed
Who never would be missed

The vendor who is rarely true
In telling you what systems do
An equivocating generalist
I've got them on the list
They'd none of them be missed
No, none of them be missed

I've got a little list, I've got a little list

There's the double talking rep with buzzbull very hep
The epitome of couth who deals in half a truth
An obscuring verbalist
Not one we'd ever miss. I've got them on the list

The software firm that makes you squirm
With manuals in Sanskrit
And updates rare for their software
That's always lost in transit
These enterprising opportunists
They'd none of them be missed.
They'd none of them be missed

There is the consultant who, works for you
And sellers too
To get a broad perspective
But without care the conflict's there
And what is then objective?
A two-faced loyalist?
They're on my list
And none of them be missed

My list is almost done, but I must mention one
Who should at once desist from writing words like this
And if he should persist
We'll put him on the list
And he'd never once be missed, never once be missed